# PROFESSIONAL EMPLOYEES

# SOCIETY TODAY AND TOMORROW

General Editor: A. H. Halsey
*Fellow of Nuffield College and Head of the Department
of Social and Administrative Studies, Oxford*

\*

# Professional Employees

## A STUDY OF SCIENTISTS
## AND ENGINEERS

KENNETH PRANDY

FABER AND FABER LTD
24 Russell Square
London

*First published in mcmlxv*
*by Faber and Faber Limited*
*24 Russell Square London W.C.1*
*Printed in Great Britain by*
*Western Printing Services Limited Bristol*

# Acknowledgements

Special thanks are due to the members of the Institution of Metallurgists, the Engineers' Guild and the Association of Scientific Workers who co-operated in my inquiries, and to the local and national officials of these organizations who gave me their help.

I should also like to acknowledge permission to quote from the salary surveys of the Institution of Metallurgists, the Engineers' Guild, the Royal Institute of Chemistry and the Institute of Physics.

# Contents

9

# List of Tables

# Part I

# INTRODUCTION

# CHAPTER ONE

# Technologists in Industrial Society

---

The study described in this book has two main intentions. One is as a contribution to the theory of social stratification, the second as a contribution to the sociology of science. The former aim is discussed in greater detail in the following chapter, our present concern is with the latter. Scientists and engineers have been chosen for study because it is believed that they are a particularly important occupational group, or number of related groups, about whom information tends to be sadly lacking. In the main part of the study technologists (for the sake of simplicity this term will often be used to cover all scientists and engineers) are dealt with in one particular area only, that of work, and in the context of the concepts of class and status. As an introduction to this, however, it seems desirable to undertake a more general discussion of the place of technologists in modern industrial society–how the various occupational groups have developed and the ways in which they have become involved in the process of politics and the system of power.

Not so very long ago it might have been necessary to offer some justification for the statement that technologists are a particularly important group in modern society. More recently, and especially since the last war, the need for justification has considerably diminished; indeed the statement is now a commonplace, and if anything the tendency is for the importance of this group to be overstressed. The growing science-based industries, and perhaps even more the new scientific methods of warfare, have brought about this change.

Sociologists, with a few notable exceptions, have tended to be rather backward in appreciating the importance of science, technology and technologists. They have managed to keep pace with popular thought, but that is all. The sociology of science has now arrived, with its own textbooks and readers, but it has been curiously long in coming. It may seem paradoxical, but it is undoubtedly true that one of the main reasons for this delay has been the early development of the subject by one man – Karl Marx. Technology is obviously of great importance in Marxist theory, however it is interpreted. One can hardly go further than to say that 'the mode of production of material life determines the general character of the social, political and spiritual processes of life'.[1] That this may be an exaggeration of the truth is a point of view which can be legitimately held. What has been far less excusable, particularly among American sociologists, has been the tendency to ignore the relationship between technology and society altogether, in Merton's words to treat 'the connection between science and social structure as a figment of Marxist sociology'.[2] In fact, this disinclination to treat the problem seriously has meant a missed opportunity for the critics, since, as Wright Mills has pointed out, it is one of the weaknesses in Marx's theory about material base and super-structure that it fails to deal adequately with the function of science and technology as a bridge between the two.[3]

The work of Weber has provided the link between Marx and later sociologists. After his study of the relationship between Protestantism and Capitalism one of Weber's self-appointed 'next tasks' was to search out 'the significance of ascetic rationalism . . . [for] the development of philosophical and scientific empiricism, [and for] . . . technical development'.[4] It was Merton who took up this theme, and in his work showed that the same protestant ethic which favoured the growth of capitalism also made possible the development of science and its application to the needs of industry.[5]

After the work of Merton and others it is now possible to discuss the relationship of technology to society. No longer is this in terms purely of the impact of the former on the latter.

[1] K. Marx, Preface to *A Contribution to the Critique of Political Economy*, Kerr and Co., 1904, p. 11.

[2] R. K. Merton, *Social Theory and Social Structure*, Free Press, 1957, p. 533.

[3] C. Wright Mills, *The Marxists*, Penguin Books, 1963, p. 104.

[4] M. Weber, *The Protestant Ethic and the Spirit of Capitalism*, Allen and Unwin, 1952, pp. 182–3.

[5] R. K. Merton, 'Puritanism, Pietism and Science' in op. cit., pp. 574–606.

# TECHNOLOGISTS IN INDUSTRIAL SOCIETY

The process of interaction has been split into its constituent parts so that more thorough analysis can take place. In particular, studies have been made of the social influences on the development of technology through new inventions,[1] of the adoption of new techniques by industry (though this has been left largely to the economists)[2] and of the effects of changing technology on social organization, both on the small and large scale.[3]

It is natural that an interest in the relationship between science and society should reflect itself also in a greater interest in the scientists and technologists themselves. Much more important, however, has been the influence of popular concern with this group. In large measure this concern dates from the very recent past, in fact from the Second World War or, to be more precise, from the dropping of the first atomic bomb. This event demonstrated in spectacular fashion the decisive influence that science could exert on society, and it came as a shock as much to politicians and intellectuals as to the ordinary man in the street.

'Until the revelation of Hiroshima, Congressmen, like most laymen, had little reason to be much concerned with either science or scientists. The majority of them undoubtedly shared the popular conception of science as the well from which material benefits flowed in an endless stream symbolized by the familiar picture of the man in a white smock holding up a test tube to the light. As for scientists, most politicians seemed to view them either as useful tools for increasing the productive resources of industry, or as impractical visionaries and eccentric crackpots. . . . The atomic bomb changed this situation completely, forcibly thrusting science and scientists into the forefront of politicians' focus of attention. . . . Detonation of the bomb drove into people's consciousness the realization, hitherto

---

[1] For a bibliography see B. Barber, 'Sociology of Science, A Trend Report and Bibliography', *Current Sociology*, vol. 5, no. 2, 1956.

[2] For a discussion of this see V. W. Rattan, 'Usher and Schumpeter on Invention, Innovation and Technical Change', *Quarterly Journal of Economics*, vol. 73, Nov. 1959, pp. 596–606.

[3] See, for example, W. H. Scott *et al.*, *Technical Change and Industrial Relations*, Liverpool U.P., 1956.

understood by only a few laymen, that science was a major social force.'[1]

So writes an American author, who goes on to describe the different images, or stereotypes, that politicians have of scientists. Many, he believed, 'seemed to regard scientists in much the same way that primitive men regard their magician priests'. Following a similar analogy another writer concluded from a study of public opinion about science and scientists that 'if the inquisitive observer watches the worshippers and the more casual passers-by, he notices respect and appreciation, but little real curiosity and interest, and he can overhear a certain amount of distrust and apprehension expressed in subdued conversations'.[2]

This lack of curiosity and interest can be detected at two levels. There is not only the ignorance of the 'common man', for whom science is something far beyond his understanding, but what is worse, the studied ignorance of those learned in the classical disciplines and the humanities. C. P. Snow has made a similar point in his strictures on the division between the two cultures.[3] Many people have taken his words to heart, but there has been in any case a greater desire to know about science, together with more effort on the part of scientists to explain and popularize their work. The intellectual opposition to science is undoubtedly diminishing, but the danger is that it is changing into an uncritical worship. The scientist has become a glamorous personality, and the scientific career has also in the eyes of many become equally attractive. There has long been a highly influential current of thought which holds that anything practical is by nature inferior and degrading, and although its influence may be declining it is still strong. Science now is accepted, but only science of the pure sort. The very term used, with its high value loading, is indicative of the attitude. Pure, basic science, so the idea runs, is eminently useless and must therefore be decent—a fit occupation for a gentleman. If this is a caricature of influential opinion, the

[1] Harry S. Hall, 'Scientists and Politicians', reprinted in B. Barber and W. Hirsch, *The Sociology of Science*, Free Press, 1962, p. 269.

[2] Stephen B. Withey, 'Public Opinion about Science and Scientists', reprinted in Barber and Hirsch, op. cit., p. 159.

[3] C. P. Snow, *The Two Cultures and the Scientific Revolution*, the Rede Lecture 1959, Cambridge U.P., 1959.

scientists themselves are partly to blame for it. They have emphasized the importance of basic research—science for its own sake—partly in order to maintain control over their own subjects, since clearly only they are competent to judge the value of such research. Once they attempt to be practical, however, they surrender judgement and therefore also direction into the hands of laymen.

At the same time, since scientists as a group are not gentlemen of leisure but have to earn their living, they always have to temper their zeal for basic research with reminders that this may eventually have results of tremendous practical importance, and they point to atomic physics as an awesome example. However, they can be excused these occasional lapses since, after all, their intentions are honourable. The full force of ignorance, misunderstanding and social disapproval is reserved for the practical men, the technologists, especially the engineers. Even though science has now become an attractive career, engineering, on the whole, has not,[1] and despite the present great demand for higher education there are quite often unfilled places in engineering departments not only in the technical colleges but even in the universities. Quite apart from other consequences these attitudes are likely to create many dissatisfied scientists, since opportunities for pursuing basic research are limited. Indeed, the distinction between pure and applied research is becoming increasingly difficult to uphold in practice.

One indication of the inferior position of engineering relative to science is the difference in social background of the practitioners. These differences in fact go back to the early periods of the two disciplines and the different ways in which they arose. Whereas science was strongly associated with the activities of gentlemen amateurs,[2] engineering has always been a practical matter, only recently becoming an academic discipline (or rather cluster of disciplines). Traditionally, the training of engineers has been largely 'on the job'. Nevertheless, although the differences existed they did not prevent a great deal of

[1] For example, those taking up engineering have lower 'A' level results than those taking up science. See *Technology and the Sixth Form Boy*, Oxford University Department of Education, 1961.

[2] See D. S. L. Cardwell, *The Organisation of Science in England*, Heinemann, 1957, p. 12.

interest in practical problems by scientists. With the rise of professional scientists and a greater theoretical emphasis in science, associated to some extent with its pursuit within the universities, this practical interest diminished, and applied science, technology and engineering, assumed a definitely inferior position, looked down upon as much by the new pure scientific culture as by the old literary one. Having been largely rejected by the universities technologists have had to be content almost until the present day with second-class educational institutions. Even now many engineers have learned their skill by some form of apprenticeship with part-time further education, and only about one-half are graduates. This contrasts markedly with the situation in science, where it is only comparatively recently that the Royal Institute of Chemistry, for example, has provided a means of professional qualification outside the university. There can be little doubt that in Britain these differences in training are both a reflection of social background and a determinant of the relative social prestige of scientists and engineers.

The whole problem of social attitudes towards science and engineering is clearly of more than academic interest. Ours is an industrial society, and if it is to maintain or improve the material standards of its members it is essential that industry becomes ever more prepared to use the skills of scientists and engineers in the right ways. It also means that these people should be produced in the right quantity and of the proper quality.

This is no new problem in Britain. It is only at the present time, if at all, that there has been a sufficient awareness of the need and an attempt made to ensure that enough trained technologists are provided. Despite the early lead in industrialization (or perhaps because of it) and the undoubted brilliance of gifted individuals, there has been a constant lag in the introduction of new industrial techniques. In the nineteenth century France and Germany, envious of Britain's lead, were much more willing to develop the industrial potential of new scientific discoveries. Although Cardwell attributes the first step in the invention of applied science to France, there is no doubt that the second, and by far the greater, was made by Germany. That country had no very great advantage, for example, in the discovery of aniline dyes, perhaps the opposite, but they showed themselves far more willing to found a new industry on the basis of this discovery. A major reason for this was that, as Cardwell says, there was 'behind the industrial scene the great educational system of the country',[1] which ensured the supply not merely of gifted individuals but also of the large number of trained technologists needed to use and to develop new techniques.

The chemical industry, and in the early stages particularly the dye industry, is the first example of the widespread application of science. Naturally, the industry was not completely neglected in Britain, but it undoubtedly lagged behind that in Germany. In large part this was a result of the quite inadequate provision for technical education. As even *The Times* once said, 'the chemical industry owes nothing to the historic educational institutions of this country'[2]—nor, one might add, much to any non-historic ones. There is a good deal of truth in the assertion that 'here we tried to start chemical industries practically without chemists'.[3] Another, associated reason was the attitudes held by those who made the decisions in industry. It was not, for example, until 1892 that the first research laboratory was set up in the chemical industry, and even then was seen as a revolutionary step, consisting as it did of 'half a dozen chemists, a general handyman and a confidential clerk'.[4] It may be noted that both the Chief Chemist of the concern which set up the laboratory and the first applicant for a post in it were Swiss.

Nevertheless, although the chemical industry in Britain lagged behind that in Germany, its growth was quite substantial. Most of the improvements which brought about the advance were made by experienced manufacturers, often themselves trained in chemistry, rather than by research chemists. Chemicals as a modern science-based industry only developed, in Britain at least, when the twentieth century was already a couple of decades old. In 1902, for example, the British Association estimated from a survey that there were some 1,500 chemists in British industry, of whom only 225 were graduates.[5]

[1] Ibid., p. 136.
[2] In 1902. Quoted in D. W. F. Hardie, *A History of the Chemical Industry in Widnes*, I.C.I. Ltd., 1950, p. 176.
[3] Quoted in Cardwell, op. cit., p. 147.     [4] Hardie op. cit., p. 176.
[5] See R. M. Pike, *The Growth of Scientific Institutions and Employment of Natural Science Graduates in Britain 1900–1960*, unpublished M.Sc. thesis, London, 1961, Chapter 1.

# TECHNOLOGISTS IN INDUSTRIAL SOCIETY

Nor can the blame for these low numbers be entirely laid on industry. If industrialists saw little point in recruiting chemists, the chemists themselves, it seems, were equally averse to working in industry–'trade' was still very much *infra dig*.

After the First World War the pace of expansion quickened, and between 1920 and 1938 the number of research chemists and the amount spent on research quadrupled. Even so there was some unemployment amongst chemists. Industry was willing to take the first-class research men, but had little use for the remainder. It took the Second World War and post-war conditions to create a 'shortage' of chemists.

The electrical industry, in all its aspects, was more obviously science-based from the beginning. The earliest industrial application of electricity, that of telegraphy, created only a fairly small demand for technologists. Subsequent expansion in this field has been steady, but even with the development of broadcasting the demand has not been very great. It is only since the Second World War that the growth of the electronics industry has stimulated a vastly increased need not only for telecommunications and electronic engineers (developed from telegraph and radio engineers) but also for physicists, who were now employed for the first time on a large scale in industry.

The other branch of the electrical industry, with its two sides of the generation of power and the machinery and appliances that make use of it, has been much more important in the demand for technological manpower. Electricity generation, as Ashworth says, 'was probably the most notable late nineteenth-century example of the influence of technology in the creation of new industry',[1] although here again development was neither smooth nor rapid–'in this combination of missed chances and great, novel achievements the history of power equipment seems very typical of the history of the techniques of British industry generally in this period' (i.e. around the turn of the century).[2] As early as 1907 14 per cent of the output of the engineering industry was electrical. Electrical engineers were demanded especially on the generating side, but were also needed by manufacturing industry for development and design work.

In the history of the growing demand for scientists and en-

[1] W. Ashworth, *An Economic History of England*, Methuen, 1960, p. 79.
[2] Ibid., p. 86.

gineers the Second World War can be clearly seen as a watershed. In the latter part of the nineteenth century discussion about technical manpower centred on the two aspects that not enough men were being trained and that industry was too slow to use those who were available. During the first third of the present century training improved considerably, so much so that despite the great increase in the employment of technologists there was, if anything, a certain amount of underemployment. But since 1945, despite a great increase in the numbers trained, the stress is on the shortage of qualified personnel. There can be little doubt that demand has grown substantially. The science-based industries have become much more important as a result of wartime and post-war developments—electronics, aircraft, petro-chemicals and atomic energy particularly—and other more traditional industries have also seen the need for scientists and engineers. At the same time the role of the government as an employer has also grown in importance. The stimulus for this advance has come partly from an increasing rate of technological innovation,[1] partly from full employment, but in part also from certain political considerations, to which we shall return.

There is now undoubtedly a far greater concern about scientific manpower and the use made of it. There exists a permanent Advisory Council on Scientific Policy with a Committee on Scientific Manpower, which has now issued several reports, and which has been incorporated into the sphere of competence of the Minister for Science. Despite the official pronouncements of this body, however, arguments still rage over the question of whether there is a shortage of scientists and engineers. The reports seem to show that there are some areas where supply is short, but that on the whole it is not great and that, moreover, by 1970 there should be if anything an excess.[2] This opinion is by no means widely shared, however, and *The New Scientist*, for example, tends to see it as merely another example of British complacency over scientific matters. Economists, also, have

[1] According to one writer the growth is exponential with a doubling every 10–15 years. See D. J. Price, 'The Exponential Curve of Science', reprinted in Barber and Hirsch, op. cit., p. 517.

[2] Advisory Council on Scientific Policy, Committee on Scientific Manpower, Statistics Committee, *The Long-Term Demand for Scientific Manpower*, Cmnd. 1490, H.M.S.O., 1961.

entered the discussion, some pointing out that the price paid for technologists has risen in response to excess demand, though with a lag,[1] others maintaining that the 'shortage' is more apparent than real, and that what is meant is that there is actually an 'unmet need', a much more difficult concept.[2]

This problem of unmet need brings us back to the question of the use made by industry of science. There may be little room to criticize the science-based industries themselves, but many of the others seem very loath either to engage in research and development or indeed to make use of what has already been done. Much of the impetus in setting up the Research Associations has come from the state, which is constantly trying in many ways to persuade industry of the value of science through the D.S.I.R. and other bodies. The Trend Report[3] is but the latest example of this.

The reason for this in the past has been the fear of technological backwardness which would put the country at a commercial disadvantage compared with other countries, particularly Germany and the United States. The motives, however, have not been purely economic. In the early days of the chemical industry, Germany was seen as the main competitor, and there can be little doubt that a large component in the fears aroused was political, the threat of dominance. The United States, perhaps for other reasons as well, was never feared in quite the same way, even though that country was even more superior technologically. At the present time, although some emphasis is laid on our position *vis-à-vis* the German and American competitors, the main point made is that Britain and 'the West' must not fall behind in the 'race' with Russia. Economics are inevitably involved in this way in international politics, and since science now plays so important a role in industry it means that science, and thereby scientists, are also brought into the same international political arena.

However, science does not merely play a greater role in

---

[1] K. J. Arrow and W. M. Capron, 'Dynamic Shortages and Price Rises—the engineer-scientist case', *Quarterly Journal of Economics*, vol. 73, May 1959, pp. 292–308.

[2] See, for example, the report of the speech by Professor Jewkes at the 1957 meeting of the B.A.A.S. in the *Economist*, vol. 192, pp. 845–6.

[3] Committee of Enquiry into the Organization of Civil Science, *Report*, Cmnd. 2171, H.M.S.O., 1963.

industry, its importance in the techniques of war is as great or even greater. Thus there have been two reasons why science has become deeply involved in politics; the old commercial one, with its political overtones, and the new one of the era of scientific warfare, with the overshadowing importance of nuclear weapons. It is of some significance that the chairman of the Committee on Scientific Manpower is Sir Solly Zuckerman, who is also Scientific Adviser to the Ministry of Defence. As he has said himself: 'This war was the turning point. Whereas previously scientists were seen, according to the interests of the observer, either as dedicated scholars, or as the source of invention, or as the technical guardians of the social services on which an urban civilization depends, today they also appear in a number of new guises—as the backbone of national defence; as pioneers of outer space; and even as the councillors of presidents and prime ministers.'[1]

The 'even' in the last phrase is significant. In a world in which science has now presented us with the means of our own total destruction, to say nothing of its less spectacular gifts, an eminent scientist expresses an element of surprise that politicians should take advice from scientists. The statement raises a very important problem. If science is so vital for modern society, for either its 'life' or its 'death', and if scientists control the development of science and technologists its application, what part do scientists, as individuals, play in making decisions about our society? Are they becoming, as Veblen prophesied, the élite of our society, or is their role merely one of being 'even' councillors of presidents and prime ministers? Do they, in short, wield power; do they even exercise very much influence?

Our knowledge about this important problem is lamentably slight, but there are some suggestive indications. It has been pointed out, for example, that in 1961, of 20 members of the cabinet 1 was a scientist (in the widest sense), of 22 permanent heads of government departments 2 were scientists, and of 20 heads of national newspapers none were scientists.[2] These figures hardly suggest very much involvement in the centres of power in Great Britain. Even more illuminating, perhaps, is the comment of an 'eminent' Fellow of the Royal Society,

[1] 'Liberty in an Age of Science', *Nature*, 18 July 1959, quoted in A. Sampson, *Anatomy of Britain*, Hodder and Stoughton, p. 509.
[2] Ibid., p. 510.

quoted by Anthony Sampson. He said of this supreme scientific body that 'they had the choice after the war of remaining a mutual admiration society, or really taking part in the control of science. They chose the former. They threw away the handles of power.'[1]

Nevertheless, scientists are not quite without influence. In his study of the relationship between government and science in the U.S.A., Price argues that many policy decisions depend upon research already completed and that 'in the long run this system, or lack of system, gives a great deal of influence in public affairs to men whose positions enable them to maintain a comprehensive view of new scientific developments', that is, 'scientists who are leaders in their professional societies and research councils'.[2]

Some of the differences between this point of view and that presented in the preceding paragraph can be explained by the fact that one refers to Britain and the other to America, but not all. It would seem that Price's argument does not stand up very well to some of the facts that he himself presents—for example, that whereas in 1938 only one-fifth of federal money spent on science was for military research, in 1953 nine-tenths was used for this purpose. Men other than scientists surely made the decisions which brought about this state of affairs.

Of course scientists are used to giving advice. C. P. Snow in his Harvard lectures has described the parts played by Tizard and Lindemann in determining strategy during the Second World War.[3] More recently there have been others, such as Sir William Penney and Sir Solly Zuckerman, who has already been mentioned.

It may thus be true that a small number of scientific advisers are influential, but as we have suggested, two questions remain. First, how influential, and second, how representative are they? Snow's lectures are a plea for scientific advice to government to be far more representative, and the story of Tizard and Lindemann is a warning of how a scientist can become immensely influential, even in non-scientific matters,[4] whilst being quite

[1] Ibid., p. 514.
[2] Don K. Price, *Government and Science*, New York U.P., 1954, pp. 28–29.
[3] C. P. Snow, *Science and Government*, Oxford U.P., 1961.
[4] In economic questions, for example. See R. F. Harrod, *The Prof*, Macmillan, 1959, p. 179.

out of touch with general scientific feeling. No single person can be a good scientific adviser, if only because he cannot separate his expert judgements from his own opinions on policy. In his excellent discussion of this problem[1] Werner Schilling states that 'the scientist, in short, is not likely to orbit the centers of political power emitting upon request "beeps" of purely technical information. He will inevitably be pulled into the political arena.'

This author nevertheless sees the role of the scientist as little different from that of any other expert in (American) government. He describes the various predispositions to which scientists as advisers are particularly prone. They have, it seems, a predilection towards naïve utopianism or naïve belligerency ('impatient optimism' in Snow's words), towards dealing with whole problems rather than with their allotted fragments, towards quantum jumps rather than piecemeal improvements (e.g. developing new weapons instead of improving old ones), towards 'technology for its own sweet sake', towards a 'sense of paradise lost', and a belief that 'science serves mankind'. These are seen as a result of the character of their expertise, although any individual scientist may exhibit none of them.

Schilling concludes, with the example of the development of radar in Britain, that 'British scientists and science were in the final measure but ready tools. They were good tools, but the use to which they were put was the result of the kind of ideas the military men had about war. The contributions that science and technology will bring to international politics will largely turn, not so much on the particular arrangements of scientists in the policy-making process, but on the purposes of statesmen and the theories they have about the political world in which they live.'

For the most part, then, scientists seem to exert influence only as tools, as technical-problem-solving machines, as superior, or perhaps rather, inferior computers. The more government relies on one individual the less true this will be. The more scientists as a whole are consulted the more likely it is to be the case. The scientists themselves seem to be content to be represented either by a very few individuals, as witness the attitude of the Royal Society, or to be used as tools of someone else's policy. This

[1] W. R. Schilling, 'Scientists, Foreign Policy, and Politics', *American Political Science Review*, vol. 56, June 1962, pp. 287–300.

traditional attitude of the divorce of values (the basis of politics) from technical expertise suffered a setback in the early days of atomic weapons, when, for example, many scientists within the Manhattan project felt a troubled concern. 'It raised no moral question about the rightness of their own actions in the realization of the atomic bomb, but it insisted that their will be consulted about its applications.'[1] This basic concern soon meant that 'problems had to be pursued into areas of social life which might have appeared earlier to be unconnected with the interests of responsible scientists'. However, this scientists' movement, and the Pugwash conferences which are another manifestation of a similar feeling, have never had the backing of the mass of technologists, nor has their influence on government policy been very great.

Many more scientists are used, and more money spent on research, for defence work than for any other activity. If their influence in this area is weak, it is no less so in others. There is doubt about the influence of scientists in the 'office of the Minister of Science', and further doubt about the influence of the Minister himself.[2] Outside the government and within industry the position is no better and may be worse. The technologist has a good chance of reaching the ranks of management, and in certain cases even the board of directors (see Chapter 3), but there is a widespread feeling that their numbers are far too few and their influence far too small.

How much influence technologists have is a question of fact; whether it is too much or too little is largely one of value, though it depends also on the factual question of how best to arrange matters so as to obtain a particular desired end in government or industry. From whatever point of view one approaches the problem, however, the necessity of studying technologists and of increasing our store of knowledge about them can hardly be disputed.

The decisions of engineers, says Merton, 'do not merely affect the methods of production. They are inescapable social decisions affecting the routines and satisfactions of men at work on the machine and, in their larger reaches, shaping the very

[1] E. Shils, 'Freedom and Influence: Observations on the Scientists' Movement in the United States', reprinted in L. J. Gould and E. W. Steele, *People, Power and Politics*, Random House, 1961, pp. 635–40.

[2] Sampson, op. cit., p. 527.

organization of the economy and society.' 'The central role of engineers as the General Staff of our productive system only underscores the great importance of their social and political orientations: the social strata with which they identify themselves; the texture of group loyalties woven by their economic position and their occupational careers; the groups to whom they look for direction; the types of social affects of their work which they take into account—in short, only by exploring the entire range of their allegiances, perspectives, and concerns can engineers achieve that self-clarification of their social role which makes for fully responsible participation in society.'[1] He suggests that it is the task of the sociologist to carry out this exploration.

No single study can hope to meet all these requirements, and the present one does not set out to do so. It is concerned only with one aspect, albeit an important one, of the 'entire range of allegiances'. The area of this concentration, and the theoretical background to it, are set out in the following chapter.

[1] R. K. Merton, 'The Machine, the Worker and the Engineer' in op. cit., p. 567.

# CHAPTER TWO

# Class, Status and Professionalism

So far we have argued the importance of studying scientists and engineers, or technologists, as a group within modern society, because of the influential position that they occupy. Any such study, however, if it is to be of real value, cannot be content merely with description and fact-finding. It must be carried out within a theoretical framework, and it should be designed to seek out such facts as enable the hypotheses derived from the theory to be tested.

The present study is concerned with only one aspect of the social situation and behaviour of technologists – that related to the way in which they are employed. More specifically it deals with their place in the authority and prestige structures, in other words the stratification system, of British industry.[1] It has the complementary aims, first, of presenting the facts of the technologists' situation in the light of a theoretical framework which should help to make them comprehensible, and second, of using these facts in order to test the theory itself. In short,

[1] The stratification system of industry is not, of course, identical to that in the wider society, and there is considerable disagreement on the question of how far the two are related. Despite the arguments about 'institutional isolation' in modern industrial societies (see R. Dahrendorf, *Class and Class Conflict in Industrial Society*, Routledge, 1959, especially pp. 267 ff.), relationships within industry must be considered as being highly important, not only in themselves but as sources of stratification in other areas. Apart from the authors discussed below in the text, emphasis on employment and occupation is to be found also, for example, in the different varieties of the 'social grading of occupations' (see the early article by J. Hall and D. Caradog Jones, 'Social Grading of Occupations', *British Journal of Sociology*, vol. 1, no. 1, March 1950), and even in Warner's system (though class for him involves 'something more' than just occupation – L. Warner and Lunt, *The Social Life of a Modern Community*, Yale U.P., 1955, pp. 81–91).

the intention is both to further our understanding of the social position of scientists and engineers and to refine the theory of social stratification.

Purely from the point of view of theory it would matter little which occupational group or groups were chosen for attention, but quite apart from the intrinsic value of studying scientists and engineers there are other good reasons why this group should be used in such a study as this. Firstly, although they are in several respects a fairly homogeneous group (in terms of education, qualification and social prestige,[1] for example), there is within this group a wide variety of employment experience—whom they work for and what sort of work they do—from engineers in high management positions to scientists in research laboratories and to those electrical engineers in the electronics industry whose work is very close to actual production. This variety enables one to make comparisons between the behaviour of similar people in different situations, and thus to suggest relationships between situation and behaviour.

A second reason why scientists and engineers are useful subjects from the point of view of theory is that they are middle class. The value of this particular attribute may not be immediately obvious, and can only be fully explained in the theoretical discussion that follows. Suffice it to say for the moment that this is a particularly suitable group in which to observe the effects of conflicting pulls and pressures. In the case of technologists the conflict is heightened by the fact that the great majority of them are, at the same time, professional people, which involves them in one set of ideas and attitudes, and employees, which involves them in a quite different set.

Allied to this last point is the third reason why technologists are particularly good subjects. The two sets of ideas and attitudes do not just exist in individuals; they are, as it were, institutionalized into two different types of organization—professional associations and trade unions—and are made more substantial in their professed aims and their activities. Before going on to a fuller discussion of the nature of these bodies,

---

[1] In an occupation rating scale based on that of North and Hatt, scientists and engineers (in America, but the position is much the same in Britain) are ranked higher than accountants and proprietors, about level with large corporation board members and architects, but lower than doctors and clergymen. See L. Reissman, *Class in American Society*, Free Press, 1959, p. 58.

however, it will be necessary to introduce the concepts and the theory of social stratification that we shall be using.

## CLASS

The concept of social class as used in this study is derived largely from the work of Karl Marx, although of course it has been refined and added to by later sociologists. Foremost among the latter is Max Weber, whose ideas on social stratification are now widely known and taught. Despite this, there seems to be a good deal of truth in Reissman's assertion that 'few theories and fewer research designs have done anything with Weber's system',[1] even if it is perhaps more applicable to sociology in America than in this country. The neglect may be explained partly by the fact that so much of Weber's theory is derived from that of Marx, being, as Gerth and Mills put it, 'an attempt to round out Marx's economic materialism by a political and military materialism',[2] and, as Reissman adds, also 'to "round out" Marx's theory by a more systematic emphasis on the social psychological elements that Marx had underplayed'.[3]

Nowhere in Marx's own writings is there a comprehensive statement and discussion of his theory of social class. The outline is reasonably clear, but many details are obscure, perhaps because Marx was too much concerned with the overall historical view to pay sufficient attention to what he thought of as the transient peculiarities of the class structure in capitalist society. The major omission was a consideration of the middle class, a weakness upon which most critics have laid great stress. Marx was not unaware of the existence of the middle class; in one work indeed he makes the criticism of Ricardo that 'what [he] forgets to mention is the continual increase in numbers of the middle classes', who 'rest with all their weight upon the working class and at the same time increase the social security and power of the upper class'.[4] On the other hand he often seems to be predicting the decline of the middle class, for example

[1] L. Reissman, op. cit., p. 58.

[2] H. H. Gerth and C. Wright Mills, *From Max Weber*, Routledge, 1948, p. 47.

[3] L. Reissman, op. cit., p. 57.

[4] K. Marx, *Theorien über den Mehrwert*, reproduced in T. B. Bottomore and M. Rubel, *Karl Marx, Selected Writings in Sociology and Social Philosophy*, Watts, 1956, p. 190.

in his statement that 'the lower strata of the middle class . . . sink gradually into the proletariat'.[1] These quotations serve to illustrate the obscurity of Marx's writings on this point, but the reason why he paid little attention to the middle class is really not hard to find. It is that it has no place in his theory of social change, to which his theory of social class is so closely bound. For the course of history only two classes are of any importance. Nevertheless, this omission weakens the utility of the theory for explaining the behaviour of middle-class groups such as technologists in modern society.

Marx saw class relationships in any society as deriving from the system of production, the method by which the means of production and labour power are brought together. In capitalist society the division is between the bourgeoisie and the proletariat, the owners of capital and the propertyless, employers and employees. Class relationships are inherently ones of conflict, for the interests of the two groups are opposed and incompatible. Such a relationship is therefore qualitatively different from other differences between groups, which arise from the division of labour. The fact of conflict in the class relationship is central to an understanding of the whole society, and is the means of social change. This latter aspect of class, its connection with social change, is not a part of our present concern, but two points need to be made in connection with it. Firstly, it may be obvious that the study, by concerning itself solely with relations within industry, implicitly rejects the revolutionary emphasis in Marx's theory. Class conflict may be acute, it may in some circumstances lead to revolution, but to insist that it must always do so is surely an unnecessary restriction of a potentially fruitful concept. It seems much more useful to accept that class conflict may be more or less acute, and may even in some cases become institutionalized.[2] Secondly, in view of the social changes which have taken place since Marx's time it is necessary to question his emphasis on the ownership of property, or rather capital, as the basis of social class under capitalism. Again there is no need to deny the partial truth of Marx's theory, but to accept that it is only partial. The ownership of capital may be one of the bases of social class, but as

[1] K. Marx, *Manifesto of the Communist Party*, Foreign Languages Publishing House, p. 59.
[2] See Dahrendorf, op. cit., p. 134, for a discussion of this.

# CLASS, STATUS AND PROFESSIONALISM

Dahrendorf has shown, there are many good reasons for treating this as one example of a more general class situation, the division between those with and those without power, irrespective of whether this power is economic or not.[1]

The concept of social class has both an objective and a subjective aspect. Marx himself saw that the objective fact of class position was something very different from the consciousness of the fact. The first would give classes 'in themselves', but it was only with a realization of common position and an acceptance of collective action that these would become classes 'for themselves'. The main factor in the growth of class consciousness, he believed, was the nature of capitalist industrial organization: 'Large-scale industry assembles in one place a crowd of people who are unknown to each other. Competition divides their interests. But the maintenance of their wages, this common interest which they have against their employer, brings them together again in the same idea of resistance—combination.'[2] It was not only that the consciousness led to collective action, but that this itself enhanced the class consciousness.

## STATUS

Under certain circumstances, therefore, the subjective consciousness of class can emerge from the objective fact. It is more difficult to understand a consciousness which seems to be at variance with the objective class position, a situation for which the term 'false class consciousness' has been used. There are many groups in modern society to whom it has been applied, particularly those members of the middle class who are salaried employees, which includes the great majority of technologists. As Lockwood says, for instance, 'the clerk is, like the manual worker, propertyless, contractual labour; in Marxian terminology, "proletarian"',[3] yet he does not feel himself a member of, or at one with, the working class, indeed usually

[1] This also avoids having to answer the question which Dahrendorf raises (op. cit., p. 21) of whether modern Britain can be considered a capitalist society.

[2] K. Marx, *The Poverty of Philosophy*, reproduced in T. B. Bottomore and M. Rubel, op. cit., pp. 186–7.

[3] D. Lockwood, *The Blackcoated Worker*, Allen and Unwin, 1958, p. 14.

34

# CLASS, STATUS AND PROFESSIONALISM

calls himself middle class. The concept of false class consciousness, as Lockwood shows, is valueless as an explanation. In
fact, such consciousness as is exhibited by these groups has little
to do with class in the Marxian sense. They do not 'believe in'
class, certainly not in any way which involves class conflict. The
idea of false class consciousness suggests that these people have
taken the wrong 'side', when really they do not think in terms
of 'sides' at all.

Class theories of stratification cannot deal adequately with
these middle-class groups, for the concern of such people is
with status, a quite different form of stratification. A theory
based on the ownership of property is clearly weakest in this
respect; one based on the possession of authority and power
much less so. The latter does allow for intermediate positions in
an authority structure, but not necessarily for the differences in
ideology and behaviour which result from these. The weakness
of Marx's theory was clearly seen by Weber. He did not reject
it—he agreed that '"property" and "lack of property" are . . .
the basic categories of all class situations'[1]—but he recognized
also another system, that of status, which was based on men's
subjective opinions. Status situation 'is determined', he says, 'by
a specific, positive or negative, social estimation of honour'.[2]
'Status groups are stratified according to the principles of their
consumption of goods as represented by special "styles of
life".'[3] This last statement is an admitted oversimplification,
and in fact other criteria, besides the consumption of goods, are
found to be honorific, notably family background and occupation (even apart from the influence of this on the consumption
of goods).

## THE RELATIONSHIP BETWEEN CLASS AND STATUS

Stratification by status can be treated quite separately from
stratification by class, and has been by some sociologists,[4] but
there are many weaknesses in doing so, and it is clear that Weber
himself saw the necessity of using both concepts, even though
keeping them distinct. As he says, 'class distinctions are linked in
the most varied ways with status distinctions. Property as such

[1] H. H. Gerth and Mills, op. cit., p. 182.
[2] Ibid., p. 187.    [3] Ibid., p. 193.
[4] Warner is the most notable example, but there are many others.

35

is not always recognized as a status qualification, but in the long run it is, and with extraordinary regularity.' Of course the two are not necessarily synonymous: 'Both propertied and propertyless people can belong to the same status group'– 'this "equality" of esteem may, however, in the long run become quite precarious'.[1]

Weber recognized that there were connections between class and status, but he failed to see how they came about. Although he asserts that status is based on subjective opinions of what is honorific, he does not attempt to show whence these opinions derive. Paradoxically, since he seemed to be unaware of the idea of status, it is Marx who can best provide a solution to this problem.[2] He rejected any theory which gave ideas an independent existence, since, as he believed, 'the social being [of men] determines their consciousness'.[3] What is more, class is for him one of the most important elements in 'social being'. Thus each class creates its own ideology, its view, more or less true, of society and the world. Not all ideologies are equally accepted, however. Because of their power 'the ideas of the ruling class are, in every age, the ruling ideas'.[4] One can question, as would Weber, whether economic power is the only source of social power, whether the bourgeoisie are necessarily the 'ruling class', but one must accept the very great, even if not the overwhelming, importance of economic power. In fact, leaving this problem aside, Weber was really saying much the same sort of thing as Marx with his 'ruling ideas' when he discussed the question of the legitimation of power. The possessors of power, of whatever sort, need to have their position recognized and accepted by those without. Power legitimized as authority is both more efficient and more secure.[5]

There is no reason to think that this process is in any way one

---

[1] H. H. Gerth and Mills, *op. cit.*, p. 187.

[2] It may also be in this case, as Schumpeter says of Weber's investigations into the sociology of religions, that 'the whole of Max Weber's facts and arguments fits perfectly into Marx's system' (J. A. Schumpeter, *Capitalism, Socialism and Democracy*, Allen and Unwin, 1943, p. 11).

[3] K. Marx, Preface to *A Contribution to the Critique of Political Economy*, Kerr and Co., 1904, pp. 11–12.

[4] K. Marx, *German Ideology*, Lawrence and Wishart, 1938, p. 39.

[5] For similar analyses, see J. Rex, *Key Problems of Sociological Theory*, Routledge, 1961, Chapter VIII; and S. Ossowski, *Class Structure in the Social Consciousness*, Routledge, 1963, Chapter VI.

of cynical reasoning. The ideology of the ruling (superordinate) group will encompass a set of values which support their position, making it perfectly legitimate in their own eyes. If the rest of society, those in subordinate positions, accept these values, then their power will be seen as authority and their position secured. It is possible that Marx had some idea of this sort in mind when he spoke of false class consciousness, but the term is never really explained. In fact within the ruling ideology there can be no place for a class view of stratification. Such a concept, involving the idea of a difference of interest and therefore conflict, would appear unnatural—this could not be the way in which society was organized. Their authority is not derived from the possession of power, but on the contrary is entrusted to them because of their special fitness to exercise it. Their social position is due to their superior birth, their wealth won by honesty and diligence, their personal qualities, or such other criteria as are used in assessing status. In short, society is seen by those in power to be stratified, not on class lines, according to the possession or non-possession of power, but on lines of status, that is, a set of superior and inferior grades in which every member accepts the validity of the status criteria, and thus his own place within the hierarchy. Status stratification is essentially harmonious, in the sense that it arises out of an acceptance of the authority structure. Individuals can compete with one another to raise their own status, but the validity of the criteria by which status is measured, the bases of legitimation, is not questioned.

That stratification by both class and status is found in modern societies cannot be doubted. Unfortunately, sociologists have tended to emphasize only one or the other, often trying to prove that only one of them is real, and that the other is a sociological imposition on the facts. As Lipset and Bendix have said, 'discussions of different theories of class are often academic substitutes for a real conflict over political orientations'.[1]

Academic differences here reflect popular ones, which themselves have political connotations. The divisions are just as one would expect from the theory which is being presented here. 'The "inferior" categories of respondents predominantly respond in terms of social classes rather than strata;

[1] S. M. Lipset and R. Bendix, 'Social Status and Social Structure', *B.J.S.*, vol. 2, 1951, p. 150.

conversely, the respondents of "superior" categories have a tendency of referring more frequently to strata than to classes.'[1] Similar results have been found by others in this field.[2] Always there is the distinction between antagonistic classes and harmonious strata or status groups, or, as Centers describes it, between a 'dynamic' and a 'static' view of society.[3] It would be a mistake to see these views as mutually contradictory, or at least to imagine that individuals see them as such. Some individuals may hold entirely one or the other of them, but the great majority seem to be aware of elements of both, without necessarily making any conscious formulation. Their behaviour may derive from one view or the other, or it may differ with the situation. Nevertheless, in any particular situation, one would expect there to be a tendency for an individual's views to be either predominantly of a class or a status type.

## THE DEVELOPMENT OF CLASS CONSCIOUSNESS

The problem of class consciousness now becomes a little clearer. Class consciousness can be seen as, in fact, a consciousness of the class system, and as leading to behaviour which is associated with such a view of society. Lack of class consciousness means not that it is 'false', but that it does not exist at all. There is no identification with the wrong class, but a rejection of a class view of society in favour of a status view. It may be objected that the former is more real than the latter, being based in objective fact rather than in mere subjective judgements, but such objections subordinate sociology to philosophy or politics. For this is a good example of a situation in which what men define as real is real in its consequences, that is, in individual or group behaviour. Nor where it affects behaviour

[1] A. Willener, *Images de la société et classes sociales*, quoted in Dahrendorf, op. cit., p. 283.

[2] See for example O. A. Oeser and S. B. Hammond, *Social Structure and Personality in a City* (Routledge, 1954), especially Chapter 20, 'Self and Society'. One reason why it is not found more often is that many sociologists force respondents into a status view. This is true of the studies of the social grading of occupations, for example. The reaction to this amongst unskilled manual workers found by Young and Willmott is of interest here (M. Young and P. Willmott, 'Social Grading of Manual Workers, *B.J.S.*, vol. 7, no. 4, Dec. 1956, pp. 337–45).

[3] P. Centers, *The Psychology of Social Classes*, Princeton U.P., 1949, pp. 26 ff.

is class entirely objective, for it is quite possible for individuals in similar objective positions to define the same situation in either class or status terms and thus to act in different ways.

Such an approach to the idea of class consciousness, however, serves rather to re-state than to solve the problem. If one accepts that the status system is created out of the class system by the attempt of the superordinate group to have their power legitimized, the question still remains of under what conditions, and to what extent, there will be acceptance or rejection on the part of the subordinate group, that is, a development of class consciousness. For Marx, it was, under capitalism, the conditions of 'large-scale industry' which would encourage this, and it is still these conditions, with refinements, which are seen as important. Lockwood, who in his study of clerks has made one of the most useful contributions,[1] treats the problem under the three aspects of 'market situation', 'work situation' and 'status situation'. The factors considered under the first heading are income, job-security, opportunities for promotion, and fringe benefits and other non-pecuniary advantages; under the second the 'physical and social estrangement of management' and the 'physical concentration and social identification of the workers themselves'; and under the third the effect of the differential distribution of prestige in aggravating or mollifying class feeling. This last is the most contentious. Status distinctions may well be no more than a reflection of differences in market and work situation, a view which Lockwood himself seems partially to accept. One must also allow that they may be a lagging reflection of former differences. On the other hand there do seem to be certain criteria of prestige which are to some extent independent of market and work situation, especially the distinction between manual and non-manual work.[2]

Dahrendorf[3] undertakes a much more ambitious and more theoretical analysis of the factors leading to a class orientation, or, in his terminology, the articulation of latent interests (in a class situation) into manifest interests. He distinguishes between

[1] D. Lockwood, op. cit.

[2] Even this distinction seems to be breaking down, however, as Lockwood's own work shows. Increasing automation is likely to accelerate the process.

[3] R. Dahrendorf, op. cit., especially pp. 237–40.

the conditions of organization, the intensity of class conflict (that is, the involvement of the parties), and the violence of class conflict (that is, the means used). Because of its concern with class as a universal phenomenon this analysis is less useful than Lockwood's when one is dealing with class consciousness in the single area of work relationships; nor does it have much to say about class consciousness as such. However, he makes a number of points which should be mentioned. By conditions of organization he means those factors which encourage the articulation of manifest interests in concrete associations, that is, in the present study, trade unions. There are, firstly, the technical conditions, by which are meant the existence of key personnel—founders and leaders—not only at a high level, but also, in a trade union, in the branch and the work group; and a charter, that is, a programme of action, or at least of belief. The former factor is obviously difficult to assess, but the latter is clearly important in a study of trade unions. Secondly, there are the political conditions, the existence of freedom of coalition, which Dahrendorf seems to use strictly in a national sense, but which, as will be seen, can be extended to situations within particular firms, for example. Thirdly, there are the social conditions. One of these, ease of communication, Dahrendorf assumes almost as given in modern societies, but here again he seems to be making his analysis at too high a level. Communication between work people and work groups can, and does, vary a great deal. The other, the existence of patterned rather than random recruitment, is much more easily assumed in the situations with which this study is concerned.

These conditions of organization are also important in the intensity of class conflict. Conflict is said to become more intense the more that certain conditions are present. For example, the more that classes are closed, which is clearly applicable at a detailed level to the question of possibilities for promotion. Again, the more that the distribution of authority and the distribution of rewards and facilities are superimposed, which clearly calls for a study of salary levels, the extent of relative deprivation, and the effect that temporary pressures of supply and demand may have on these.

To summarize, it would seem to be necessary to consider three elements in the development of class consciousness. Firstly, the actual class situation of an individual or group must

# CLASS, STATUS AND PROFESSIONALISM

be assessed. It is analytically useful to talk of class as deriving from the distribution of power or authority, but it must be remembered that in practice it is not always easy to draw a dividing line between those who do and those who do not possess authority. Many individuals have a certain amount of authority over others, but it is not final. They are in a position of subordination to some and superordination to others; they both exercise and are subject to authority. There are obvious difficulties in assigning such people to a particular class position. The case of the foreman in many industrial organizations indicates that the problem is a real one. Secondly, assuming that an individual or a group is in a subordinate position, there are the factors which tend to make this position more obvious or less desirable. These include those covered by Lockwood's work situation—such things as greater mechanization, routinization, and physical concentration, which emphasize the individual's separation from management and lessen his control over his work (as well as often making it intrinsically less satisfying)—and his market situation—the relative financial and other rewards, the chances of mobility, and so on. Thirdly, given the presence of the above factors, there are the conditions which allow organization to take place. Many of these, physical concentration for example, are similar to those mentioned above, but to them must be added Dahrendorf's technical, political (widely interpreted), and social conditions.

The hypothesis which emerges from these arguments, therefore, is that the more the conditions described above, poor market situation, a work situation which emphasizes the subordination to management and so on, are present in the employment experience of a group, the less its attitudes and behaviour will be of a status type, and the more they will be of a class variety. There is not necessarily a sharp change from status to class attitudes. The two ideologies are opposed only as ideal types; in practice, because of the way in which they arise, they form a continuum. An acceptance of the claims to legitimacy of the ruling group leads to the holding of a status ideology. The conditions described serve to weaken the degree of acceptance, to bring about a recognition of the conflict of interest, and thus to encourage class attitudes. However, since these conditions are present in lesser or greater degrees, it follows that the strength of status and class attitudes will vary.

41

This is why behaviour and attitudes are often described in this study as 'tending towards' one or other, and not just as being a class or a status attitude or type of behaviour.

It should now be clearer why a middle-class occupational group is so suitable for testing our hypotheses. Since they are not situated at either extreme of the class-status continuum, they are most likely to hold views and exhibit behaviour which are a mixture of the class and status types. Being in the middle they are the most obviously subject to pressures from both directions. The effect of such conflicting pressures should be demonstrated in the different behaviour and attitudes of those in differing employment situations.[1] Moreover, in the case of technologists the effect can be studied also in the aims and activities of the two types of organization that represent substantial numbers of them. Since the position of scientists and engineers in industry is best understood with reference to these bodies, we must now discuss in more detail the ways in which trade unionism and professionalism are related to the concepts of class and status respectively.

## TRADE UNIONISM

It is possible to raise doubts about the usefulness of treating trade unions as expressions of class consciousness. Lockwood, for example, believes that 'there is no inevitable connection between unionization and class consciousness'. 'Concerted action', he says, 'is a function of the recognition by the members of the occupational group that they have interests in common; class consciousness entails the further realization that certain of those interests are also shared by other groups of employees.'[2] This is a valid point, but should not be overstressed. Their existence does, after all, indicate a major break from normal, accepted middle-class values. A trade union is unlike any other occupational association in that its function is to bargain with employers on behalf of employees. In thus giving expression to a conflict of interest it is a class association,

[1] This use of the comparative method differs from that of Lockwood in his study of clerks. Whereas he compared the behaviour of the same occupational groups at different points in time, the present study compares the various sub-groups of an occupational group at the same point in time.

[2] D. Lockwood, op. cit., p. 137.

and by joining it its members have to some extent given up a large part of their status ideology in favour of a class ideology. In Lockwood's own words they realize that 'their common interests are engendered by the conflict of interest between employer and employee'. This consciousness of class is surely of great importance, even though it may not be termed class consciousness, which Lockwood sees as a realization that 'their common interests are not fundamentally dissimilar in type from those underlying the concerted actions of manual workers'.[1] Even this would in any case not satisfy some definitions of class consciousness, which would require not merely a recognition of the 'not dissimilar' interests of others, but a feeling of common interest with all members of the working class. It seems more fruitful to think of 'class consciousness' as an ideal type, which in practice can be more or less intense. If it is recognized as 'consciousness of conflict of interest', then it may be seen also as varying from 'individual' to 'group' and finally 'class' consciousness. How far even many groups of manual workers, including trade unionists, can be said to exhibit this last type is surely open to question. Any definition which suggests equal treatment in the wider society would to that extent lose in utility, since here status may be considered more important than class.

## PROFESSIONALISM

The existence of a trade union, therefore, is taken as an indication of class attitudes. The important feature of a trade union in this sense is that it is a bargaining body, a definition very much the same as that used, as a result of practical experience, by the Ministry of Labour.[2] Not all occupational associations are trade unions, and in the case of professional associations it merely creates confusion to think of them as such. Confusion undoubtedly exists in much popular thinking on the subject, so that Arnold Bennett, for example, could speak of the 'two great Trade Unions' of doctors and lawyers.[3] To some extent, if it is naïvely interpreted, the study by Caplow[4] in which he

[1] Ibid., p. 137.
[2] In its Directory of Employers' Associations, Trade Unions, etc.
[3] Quoted in G. Wallas, *Our Social Heritage*, p. 122.
[4] T. Caplow, *Sociology of Work*, Oxford U.P., 1954.

compared the activities of trade unions and professional associations might add to this. As the study shows, many of their activities are very similar, and are mainly directed to the same end of economic protection, but it is important to realize the differences in ideology which underlie the two. Trade unions are class bodies—they bargain with employers; professional associations are status bodies—they bestow a qualification and seek to maintain or enhance its prestige.

Many of the differences between them arise from the different circumstances of their members, especially the fact that trade union members are employees whilst professionals are independent practitioners. This, of course, is only to say that the former are in positions of subordination while the latter are not, and this fits in well with the present hypotheses until it is remembered that many professionals are not independent practitioners but are themselves employees. Certain of them, it is true, enjoy a semi-independent status, often doing work which still essentially involves a client-practitioner relationship in which profit or business ethics have no place. Doctors in this country are a clear example of this, and so also are judges, social workers and many others employed by central or local government. Much more difficult groups are those, like scientists and engineers, who are employed directly, especially by business organizations, without any such practitioner-client relationship; and a consideration of such groups raises the whole problem of the nature of professionalism.

There have been numerous attempts to define the terms 'profession' and 'professionalism', and almost all of them have admitted the difficulties involved. Carr-Saunders and Wilson, the authors of the fullest account of the professions in Britain, did not feel themselves able even to attempt the task, accepting the O.E.D. definition of 'a vocation in which a professed knowledge of some department of learning or science is used in its application to the affairs of others or in the practice of an art founded upon it'.[1] The difficulty with this, as with most other attempted definitions, is one of where to draw the line. The general public and individual authors have their own ideas of which groups are 'professions' and which are not, but there seems to be no satisfactory definition which will

[1] A. M. Carr-Saunders and P. A. Wilson, *The Professions*, Oxford U.P., 1933.

embrace all the former and yet exclude all the latter. The O.E.D. definition is criticized by Lewis and Maude because it would allow in too many groups who are not really in their view professional.[1] The difficulty in practice is found very much in engineering, where there are many specialized Institutions modelled very closely on the senior bodies for civil, mechanical and electrical engineers. The latter, however, will not accept their professional status because they are too specialized, whereas a 'professional engineer' must have a broad education. The judgement as to where a specialized education ends and a broad one begins can obviously be only an arbitrary one.

Any definition in terms of the existence of an association will run into similar difficulties; almost any occupational group can form an association. They may thereby claim professional status, but their claim need not be accepted. Most authors have in fact recognized the inadequacy of this type of definition and have usually tended to stress rather more the values which are involved in the idea of professionalism. In the main these values are clustered around two concerns. The first is the desire of the profession to hallmark the competent. Those who use the services are thus given a guarantee that the individual at least ought to be able to perform certain tasks adequately. Here again there is the obvious difficulty that any association can bestow qualifications, so that it is really the second set of values which must be emphasized. These guarantee the integrity of the members by requiring from them a strict adherence to a defined code of conduct, with expulsion as a final sanction. It is this which is most often seen as the essence of professionalism. Lewis and Maude come to the conclusion that 'a moral code is the basis of professionalism',[2] and Kaye, who says in the introduction to his study of architects that 'a profession may be defined as an occupation possessing a skilled intellectual technique, a voluntary association and a code of conduct,' emphasizes that 'it is this last factor, the guarantee of integrity, that is the main distinguishing mark of the professions'.[3]

[1] R. Lewis and A. Maude, *Professional People*, Phoenix, 1952. 'But if the position is yielded, as it is in the Carr-Saunders definition, then ultimately men and women of the smallest learning and slenderest academic resources must be conceded professional status—foremen and works supervisors, for example' (p. 57).    [2] Ibid., p. 64.

[3] B. Kaye, *The Development of the Architectural Profession in Britain*, Allen and Unwin, 1960, p. 17.

# CLASS, STATUS AND PROFESSIONALISM

It is no argument against the importance of a moral code to show that the motives inspiring it are not necessarily altruistic. In the case of independent professionals altruism and self-interest are happily combined. Parsons has made the point that the principles of commercialism and professionalism are not wholly dissimilar, and that they are designed to attain much the same result.[1] There are other more important objections, however. The first is that this definition still does not satisfactorily solve the problem of the 'pretenders', who could devise and strictly enforce a moral code. Put this way there is in fact no solution to the problem. It exists not in sociology but in popular thinking. The label 'professional' has become one of prestige and status, and the problem has arisen out of a desire to prevent groups of lower status from assuming this prestige label. The sociological solution is clear; if such groups behave in all ways like other professionals then it is best to treat them as such. This is not to say that the sociologist should not look at what groups actually do, rather than at what they say or think they do, but it is to recognize the most important fact about such groups—that their behaviour is motivated by a status ideology.

The second objection is more vital. The importance of the code of conduct for independent professionals need not be disputed, but one can question how far it is applicable to those professionals who are employees. Of course they must be honest and diligent, but so must any other employee; as Lewis and Maude write, 'good service to an employer is not exclusively part of the professional code; it is the condition of employment at the ruling salary'.[2] The sanction, as with any other employee, is not expulsion from the professional group but dismissal by the employer. The authors just quoted try to retrieve the position somewhat, and feel that whilst 'the extent to which a professional ethic can be said to exist among employed persons is limited', nevertheless 'with professional status goes a high sense of duty towards the employer'.[3] The weakness of the argument is obvious, and they have really already answered it themselves, but there is something in it. The high sense of duty is part of a status ideology which can exist quite independently of professionalism. The professional

---

[1] T. Parsons, 'The Professions and Social Structure', in *Essays in Sociological Theory*, Free Press, 1954.

[2] R. Lewis and A. Maude, op. cit., p. 62.　　　　　　[3] Ibid., p. 63.

association is important as a concrete expression of this ideology among certain groups. In theory such people may not be properly professional, but in practice that is how they see themselves. The latter will obviously affect their behaviour, but it cannot do so alone. The theory is based in reality, and it is necessary to look for ways in which this reality affects, first of all, behaviour and, secondly, the individual's self-perceptions.

Such theoretical considerations determine the form of this study. Basically the intention is to show how the differing employment situations in which scientists and engineers are placed influence their attitudes and behaviour in the direction of a class or a status ideology, represented on the one hand by trade unions and on the other by professional associations. There are also several sub-themes; firstly a consideration of the nature of professionalism amongst this group, how near it is to the ideal of professionalism, and how far employees such as technologists can be considered as professionals; secondly, a consideration of how far there is a confusion of ideologies—status elements in trade unions and class elements in professional associations. The study thus falls into three main parts; firstly, as a background, a general description of the employment of scientists and engineers; secondly, a consideration of professionalism, with a discussion of the aims and activities of all the professional associations in this field, followed by a study of the attitudes of the members of an accepted professional association and of the members of a small body which attempts to provide professional protection without any of the other functions (which should be of interest in showing the particular difficulties of professional employees); thirdly, an assessment of the different trade unions which recruit in this field, and a study of the background and attitudes of the members of one of the more important of them. Thus, with the information gained from the first part, the second attempts to show how the professional bodies for scientists and engineers are related to a status ideology, and how different employment situations encourage class attitudes. The third part then pursues the matter further, by showing which sorts of employment conditions have led to unionization.

47

# CHAPTER THREE

# The Employment of Technologists

Having briefly described the development of employment for scientists and engineers in the first chapter, it is useful at this point to present more detailed information on the areas in which technologists are employed, the type of work they do, and the salaries they receive. This should serve to provide a background against which the findings of the study can be set. At certain points, unfortunately, this background is somewhat blurred. Through the work of the Advisory Council on Scientific Policy a great deal is known globally about the numbers of the different types of technologists and the industries in which they are employed, but there is still a lack of information about the type of work that scientists and engineers perform and of their typical career patterns.

## AREAS OF EMPLOYMENT

The Advisory Council on Scientific Policy has so far issued three reports on scientific and engineering manpower in Great Britain.[1] According to the latest of these, there were, in 1962, 185,194 qualified[2] scientists and engineers working in Britain. Of these, 51·9 per cent were employed in private industry, 23·9 per cent were engaged in education, 11·7 per cent were

[1] Ministry of Labour and the Advisory Council on Scientific Policy, *Scientific and Engineering Manpower in Great Britain 1956*, H.M.S.O., 1956; Advisory Council on Scientific Policy, *Scientific and Engineering Manpower in Great Britain 1959*, Cmnd. 902, H.M.S.O., 1959; *Scientific and Technological Manpower in Great Britain 1962*, Cmnd. 2146, H.M.S.O., 1963.

[2] This study uses the definition of 'qualified' given by the Advisory Council. See op. cit. (*1962*), pp. 23–24.

48

employed by the nationalized industries, 8·1 per cent by central and 4·3 per cent by local government. This overall pattern masks some very large differences between the various types of technologists. For example, nearly 79 per cent of mathematicians are in education, whereas 77 per cent of metallurgists are in private industry.

Within the field of private manufacturing industry five groups, which account for only slightly more than one-third of all employees, employ between them two-thirds of all technologists. The five groups, in order of importance as employers, are chemicals (other than oil refining), mechanical engineering, electrical engineering, aircraft and electronic apparatus. They are, as one would expect, the major employers of technologists in their respective fields—chemists in the first, mechanical engineers in the second and fourth, and electrical engineers in the third and fifth. In addition, certain of these industries are important in giving employment to other groups. The electronics industry, for example, is by far the main employer of physicists, accounting for nearly one-third of those in industry. The chemical and electrical engineering industries are also the third and fourth largest employers of mechanical engineers.

There are several industries of lesser importance in the employment of technologists. Iron and steel employs most of the metallurgists, although in absolute terms there are more mechanical engineers in this industry. The latter are found also in motor vehicles, whilst there are a substantial number of chemists in the food, drink and tobacco group. Mineral oil refining, although not a major field of employment, is remarkable for the high proportion of technologists to other employees —6·6 per cent, compared with an average of 1·3 per cent.

The construction industry is the sixth most important employer of technologists, mostly civil and structural engineers.

The largest employer amongst the nationalized industries and public corporations is the electricity supply industry. Most of these employees, naturally, are electrical engineers. The U.K. Atomic Energy Authority, unlike most other industries, does not employ any one type of technologist in overwhelming numbers. The most numerous are mechanical engineers, physicists and chemists. Not unexpectedly, perhaps, the A.E.A. has the highest ratio of technologists to other employees (13·1 per cent) of any nationalized or private industry. The other

## THE EMPLOYMENT OF TECHNOLOGISTS

substantial employers amongst the nationalized industries are the National Coal Board—mostly mining engineers, the gas industry—nearly all mechanical engineers, the G.P.O.—electrical engineers, and the British Transport Commission—civil engineers.

The central government is also an important employer of scientists and engineers. Rather more than one-half of the total technologists in the Civil Service are in Defence Departments, with roughly one-quarter each in Civil Departments and Research Councils. The main types employed are mechanical engineers, electrical engineers, physicists and chemists. The Local Authorities, although of little overall importance, employ just over 40 per cent of all civil and structural engineers.

Education—schools, technical and teacher training colleges and universities—is another major field of employment for scientists. Slightly more than 48 per cent of scientists work in educational institutions as compared with only 7 per cent of engineers. But among scientists there are large differences, ranging from the 69 per cent of biologists and 64 per cent of mathematicians to the 26 per cent of chemists.

To sum up the position from the point of view of the different specialisms, those most likely to be employed by public bodies are the civil engineers in local government, electrical engineers in the electricity supply industry, and mathematicians and physicists in education. In private industry most groups are associated mainly with one particular industry—chemicals, electrical engineering, electronics, mechanical engineering, iron and steel.

The Advisory Council on Scientific Policy has also produced a report on the estimated future employment of technologists,[1] which is of some interest. The proportions in each field are expected to remain roughly the same in the decade from 1961 to 1971, though the proportion in industry will probably rise a little, so that by 1970 there will be twice as many technologists employed in private industry as there are now. The industries with a greater demand than this will be chemicals, mineral oil refining, electrical engineering and electronics. Overall, it is expected that the ratio of technologists to other employees will

[1] Advisory Council on Scientific Policy, Committee on Scientific Manpower, Statistics Committee, *The Long-Term Demand for Scientific Manpower*, Cmnd. 1490, H.M.S.O., 1961.

## THE EMPLOYMENT OF TECHNOLOGISTS

almost double. The most significant forecast is that by 1970 the supply of scientists and engineers will be adequate to meet the demand. If this proves correct it may have some interesting effects on the general market situation for technologists and the sorts of work on which they are employed.

### TYPE OF WORK

In the latest report of the Advisory Council they describe the type of work performed by technologists under three headings – (1) research and development; (2) manufacture, production, operation, maintenance, installation and design for manufacture; (3) all other work (including management, sales, etc.). Unfortunately, they give a full definition only of the first of these divisions, so that it is not clear, for example, which category plant or production managers come into.

However, taking the categories as given, and dealing first with scientists proper, only two industrial groups are of any importance. In the first, chemicals, 47 per cent of the scientists are in research and development, a further 31 per cent are in production work (manufacture, etc.), and quite a high proportion, 22 per cent, are doing other (i.e. non-technical) work. In the second, the electronics industry, the great majority of scientists, 74 per cent, are on research and development.

The situation is somewhat different for technologists, since in general these are less likely to be engaged in research and development. The main exceptions to this are electronics, where 58 per cent come into this category, and aircraft, with 56 per cent. The two industries which have a higher proportion of their technologists in non-technical work are mechanical and electrical engineering, with 26 per cent and 25 per cent respectively in this category. The former industry also has a high proportion in the production work group (54 per cent), which is significant also for technologists in chemicals (70 per cent), iron and steel (60 per cent), and electrical engineering (42 per cent).

These national figures are rather gross and somewhat difficult to interpret. A little further information can be obtained from a study made in the Manchester area. Even this, however, stated that 'scientists/technologists are employed in so many different capacities that it has been found impossible to classify them by

51

the posts they occupy'.[1] They make an exception for directors, who actually comprised nearly 10 per cent of the whole group and were found in almost 40 per cent of all the firms visited. The study distinguishes between graduates and diploma holders, that is those with professional qualifications (A.R.I.C., A.I.Mech.E., etc.) only. Those in the former category have a slightly better chance of a directorship than the latter; in fact '74 graduates out of a total of 684, or roughly one in nine, had reached board level by his own efforts unassisted by family associations', though it is perhaps significant that 'in no case covered by the survey was it found that a man who had been employed solely on research had been appointed to the board of management of his firm'.[2]

Overall, graduates were found equally distributed between research and development and other work, but where a research and development department existed they were usually employed more in this, in the ratio of 3 to 2. Individual variations were very wide, however, ranging from the firm in which 25 out of 31 graduates were employed on testing, standardization and production, and another with 47 out of 55 graduates on production and process control, to those with 70 out of 75, and 20 out of 21 graduates engaged in research and development. This study found, as also do the Advisory Council reports, that it is the larger firms which have both a higher proportion of technologists and a larger number in research and development.

Holders of diplomas had less chance than graduates (about half) of obtaining a directorship. Most of this group were to be found in the mechanical engineering, chemical and electrical engineering industries, and 87 per cent of them were in firms with over 500 employees. Only in the electrical engineering industry were there many employed on research and development. Elsewhere they were usually in management or process control.

To sum up, as far as this is possible, one can say that scientists are more likely to be in research and development than in either of the other categories, and that for technologists this category and that of production are roughly equally important, allowing for the wide variations between industries. On the

[1] Manchester Joint Research Council, *Industry and Science*, Manchester U.P., 1954, p. 23.　　　　　　　　　　　　　　[2] Ibid., p. 25.

whole, the proportions doing non-technical work, that is, mostly management, are quite large—one-fifth in some cases. The chances for scientists and engineers to reach high management positions, even a seat on the board, are fairly good. Given these promotion prospects and the relatively congenial nature of much of their work, this group would appear to be in a generally favourable work situation.

## EARNINGS

There is, fortunately, quite a lot of information available on the earnings of scientists and engineers, although not in as much detail as could be wished. It comes from the salary surveys carried out at regular intervals by the Royal Institute of Chemistry, the Institute of Physics, the Institution of Metallurgists and the Engineers' Guild.[1]

For purposes of comparison the figures given in the tables refer to the position in the period 1959–60, although some of the associations have carried out later surveys. Table 1 shows the

### TABLE 1

*Earnings of Scientists and Engineers by Age*
*(median in £'s) 1959–60*

| | Age | | | |
|---|---|---|---|---|
| | *31–35* | *41–45* | *51–55* | |
| Chemists | 1,370 | 1,850 | 2,050 | |
| | *31–35* | *41–50* | *51–60* | |
| Metallurgists‡ | 1,500* | 1,865* | 3,230† | |
| | *35* | *45* | *50* | |
| Physicists | 1,600* | 2,000* | 2,500† | |
| | *30–34* | *40–44* | *50–54* | *All ages* |
| Civil Engineers | 1,230 | 1,485 | 1,900 | 1,515 |
| Mechanical Engineers | 1,275 | 1,635 | 1,700 | 1,567 |
| Electrical Engineers | 1,255 | 1,595 | 1,840 | 1,584 |
| Chemical Engineers | 1,700 | 2,420 | 2,500 | 2,175 |

*Associates    †Fellows    ‡Average

[1] Royal Institute of Chemistry, *Remuneration Survey, 1959, 1962*; Institute of Physics, *Salary Survey–1960*, reprinted in the Bulletin of the Institute, Nov. 1960; Institution of Metallurgists, *Remuneration Survey, 1960, 1963*; Engineers' Guild, *The Professional Engineer*, vol. 6, no. 9, Jan. 1961; vol. 8, no. 6, Nov.–Dec. 1963.

annual earnings of various types of scientists and engineers in selected age-groups. The general pattern throughout the age-range is similar, but for making comparisons it is probably best to take the 31–35 group, who are the most numerous. Chemical engineers then appear to be the best paid, mostly because there are so few of them and they are very much in demand. Some way behind them are physicists, then metallurgists, chemists, mechanical, electrical and civil engineers. This is perhaps the best ranking of the overall financial attractiveness of the different specialisms at the time when these surveys were made, bearing in mind also the slight differences in the actual timing of the surveys.

Evidence from the more recent surveys shows that there have been considerable changes in the pattern of distribution between different types of technologist, generally working towards greater equality of earnings. The highly-paid chemical engineers have had a rise in median income for all ages of only 1·4 per cent between 1960 and 1963, whereas metallurgists, in the same period, have enjoyed rises of 11 per cent for Associates at age 31–35, 8 per cent at 36–40 and 13 per cent at 41–50. Chemists seem to have fared better, with increases of 19 per cent for the 31–35 age-group, 15·9 per cent for the 41–45 group and 20·5 per cent for the 51–55 group, whilst electrical engineers have had increases of 23·7 per cent and civil engineers an income rise of 29·3 per cent.

There are, of course, also differences in earnings between the various fields of employment. Unfortunately, none of the surveys gives details of differences in earnings within private industry, though on the whole the figure given will reflect the earnings of those in the major employing industry for that particular specialism.

Certain groups are employed almost entirely in one field, and this will affect their overall position. Chemical engineers and metallurgists, for example, are mostly employed in private industry, and since at the time of these surveys this tends to be a better-paying field, they are amongst the best paid. Mathematicians on the other hand, most of whom are in school-teaching, one would expect to be less well off, even though the individual mathematician in industry might earn more than the average metallurgist. In Table 2 are shown the differences in earnings between industries and fields of employment.

TABLE 2

*Earnings of Scientists and Engineers by Industry*
*(in £'s) 1959–60*

| | Engineers† (All members) | | Chemists† (All members) | | Metallurgists‡ (Associates) | |
|---|---|---|---|---|---|---|
| | *30–34* | *40–44* | *31–35* | *41–45* | *31–35* | *41–50* |
| Private Industry | 1,275 | 1,665 | 1,420 | 1,980 | 1,520 | 1,940 |
| Nationalized Industry | 1,245 | 1,445 | — | — | 1,700 | 2,125 |
| Coal | — | — | 1,220* | 1,650 | — | — |
| Gas | — | — | 1,110* | 1,490* | — | — |
| Electricity | — | — | 1,360* | 1,720* | — | — |
| U.K.A.E.A. | — | — | 1,400 | 1,950 | — | — |
| Civil Service | 1,235 | 1,475 | — | — | 1,390 | 1,650 |
| Scientific | — | — | 1,340 | 1,750 | — | — |
| Other | — | — | 1,250* | 1,790* | — | — |
| Local Authority | 1,085 | 1,300 | 1,120 | 1,590* | — | — |
| Education | | | | | | |
| University | — | — | 1,380 | 1,960 | 1,790 | 2,270 |
| Tech. College | — | — | 1,350 | 1,600 | 1,500 | 1,635 |
| School | — | — | 1,130 | 1,350 | — | — |

*Very small numbers   †Median   ‡Average

As far as engineers are concerned, although there is a slight variation in the order of financial attractiveness with age, private industry is clearly the best-paying field and local government the worst. It is because those employed by the latter are mostly civil engineers that this group tends altogether to be the worst paid. Electrical engineers constitute a majority of those employed by the nationalized industries. Even though this tends to depress their average salaries they are still, as a whole, slightly better off than mechanical engineers.

The pattern for chemists is somewhat similar, with private industry the best-paid field and with schoolteaching replacing local government, which is of no significance in the employment of chemists, as the worst.

By itself the U.K.A.E.A. pays almost as well as private industry, but other nationalized industries by no means do so. The numbers involved here, however, are few—too few, in fact, to make the figures given fully trustworthy. The universities are, for chemists, not very far below industry, especially for the older men, but the technical colleges, although they compare well for the younger group, tend to fall behind for the older ones.

Metallurgists are better paid than chemists, although the earnings shown in the table are not strictly comparable, since those for this group are average and not median. On the other hand, they refer only to Associates, and whilst the latter form a majority of the age-groups concerned, the inclusion of Fellows would further raise the figures given. For private industry alone, in which most of the metallurgists are employed, the difference is not very large, and the position of the two groups is probably very similar, but in other areas the metallurgists seem to do much better. The universities are the most lucrative field, followed by nationalized industry (in effect the U.K.A.E.A.), with the Civil Service and the technical colleges some way behind.

No detailed figures are given for physicists, but the position described is that salaries in industry are close to the general average, whilst those for the U.K.A.E.A. are £50–£100 higher. Civil Service salaries are just slightly below, and schoolmaster salaries well below—from about £150 less at 32 to £300 less at 45. For the younger Associates university salaries are far below, and those in technical colleges far above the figure for industry, but for older members the positions seem to be reversed and university salaries move nearer to those of industry.

The 1962 surveys show that this pattern has changed somewhat. For engineers, incomes in industry are lower than those in all other fields except local government. The U.K.A.E.A. is the best-paying employer for both engineers and chemists, and for the latter the technical colleges and universities are better-paying fields for the younger and older age-groups respectively. The same tendency, that is for earnings in areas other than private industry to have risen more rapidly than those in industry and even to have overtaken them, is shown also in the case of metallurgists.

Not only are there no detailed figures showing differences in earnings within private industry, there are none which would enable comparisons to be made between earnings in different types of work. The Engineers' Guild provides a certain amount of evidence in that they differentiate those engineers who are in management positions other than by virtue of being engineers. The individual manager was left to decide for himself whether he had attained his position by the fact of being an engineer or for some other reason. In many cases this would be a difficult decision to make, and the Guild anyway gives no idea of the numbers involved. However, the finding is that those who consider themselves to be in non-engineering occupations are far better paid than the remainder—a median salary of £2,714 compared with an overall figure for engineers of £1,574 or, since age may be important, of £1,778 for the 55–64, the best paid, age-group. This finding is repeated in the 1962 survey, where non-engineering occupations are again the best paid, and it would seem to support the feeling of many engineers that a successful career is the one that leads into general management.

It is interesting that a university degree is worth some £300 p.a. more for engineers than the equivalent professional qualification, i.e. corporate membership of the appropriate Institution. This may be just an extra payment for the possession of a degree, or it may be a reflection of the fact that graduates are favoured for management positions. If this is so, it may also explain why a degree is worth more for mechanical engineers (£450 p.a.—non-graduates outnumber graduates by 2·5 to 1) than for civil engineers (less than £100—graduates outnumber non-graduates by 1·5 to 1). It may be that since there are proportionately fewer graduates amongst the mechanical engineers most of them are chosen for management positions, leaving fewer in the lower-paid jobs. Other factors, especially scarcity and differences in the field of employment, may also of course enter in.

Apart from this small piece of information there is nothing to suggest which types of jobs are best paid. As with the engineers there is a feeling amongst other groups that it is the management jobs that pay most, and that, financially, research and development and production work are inferior. As was noted above, research work in fact carries fewer chances of promotion to the very top.

Differences in earnings for different types of work may, however, be cut across by differences between the types of technologists. Although the proportions engaged in research and development and in production are known for each industry they are not known for each specialism. Any inference based on these proportions, on the types of technologists employed, and on the earnings of these would be far too tenuous to be of any value. It can only be said that if the feelings of other groups are as accurate as those of engineers seem to be, then that work, research and development and production, in which the technical skills are most directly used, is less well paid than management and other mainly non-technical work.

The general conclusion that emerges from the discussion of the employment and earnings of scientists and engineers is that their work and market situations are on the whole favourable. Certain groups, a minority, will of course be in less favourable positions, and it is amongst these that trade unionism, or at least tendencies towards class attitudes, are most likely to be found. However, it is to be expected that the predominant attitudes will be of a status variety, and it is therefore to a consideration of professionalism that the study first turns.

# Part II

# PROFESSIONALISM

# Introduction

The nature of professionalism and the ideas surrounding it have already been discussed at length in the second chapter. Some of the points raised there may usefully be briefly repeated, so that they may be borne in mind in the succeeding chapters, where the activities of the professional associations for scientists and engineers and the attitudes of the members of two of them are considered.

The main point made was that it is very difficult, if not impossible, to give a definition of professionalism which would at once embrace all those who are accepted as professional whilst rejecting all those who are not. This is not to say that there are no characteristics which are not found more amongst professional groups than amongst others, the most important of these being an advanced intellectual training, a formal qualification, a code of conduct, and an association which at least takes a deep interest in, perhaps has some control over, these other matters, and is generally representative of the professional group. These characteristics of a profession will be considered in relation to scientists and engineers, with a special emphasis on the role of the professional associations in exercising their various functions. The attitudes of the members towards their associations, and particularly their opinions on the relative importance of their various functions, will also be dealt with.

A theoretically more important conclusion drawn from the fact that it is virtually impossible to give a satisfactory definition of a profession was that the attempt to do so is largely a mistaken one, and that the real point of professionalism for employees lies elsewhere. The argument put forward was that for the sociologist the main consideration was not the question of whether or not a particular group are really professionals, but the fact that they claim to be so and that they aspire to professional status. The concern with status is believed to lie at the heart of professionalism as it affects employees, being basically more important than any of the external characteristics.

The high status of professional people probably derives in great part from the early equation of professionalism with independent fee-paid practice, but of course professional status has since been extended to many groups who are not independent at all, who are in fact employees. As was argued, this has meant some strain in the ideas of professionalism for these groups. In particular, there is the possibility, in terms of the theory of social stratification put forward, that these professional employees, by pursuing the function of professional protection, may find themselves engaging in activities which are more of a class than a status type. This tendency, according to the theory, is much more likely to occur amongst, or be demanded by, those in a particular work situation, briefly, those who are low in the authority hierarchy and whose work emphasizes their subordination. Thus in surveying the activities of the associations and the attitudes of their members it is necessary not only to look for evidence of the concern with status and the means by which it is pursued, but also to look for signs of class attitudes—where, and amongst whom, they are found.

# CHAPTER FOUR

# Professional Associations

---

## HISTORICAL

The origin of the professional associations for scientists and engineers is to be found in the early nineteenth century. By this time important advances had been made in science, whilst its application to industrial and everyday domestic life was becoming more widespread. Science and technology had become matters of general concern, and this was reflected in the formation of a number of societies. As Cardwell says of the period: 'On the one hand there were the advances associated with the names of Dalton, Young, Davy, Wollaston and others and, on the other, there was the proliferation of societies and philosophical institutes.'[1] As early as 1771 the Society of Civil Engineers was formed with the idea that 'the sharp edges of their minds might be rubbed off, as it were, by a closer communication of ideas',[2] but it did not serve adequately the needs of the mainly young engineers who, in 1818, founded the Institution of Civil Engineers with the object of 'facilitating the acquirement of knowledge necessary in the civil engineering profession and for promoting mechanical philosophy'.[3] Civil engineering at this time meant all engineering that was not military, in fact 'being the art of directing the Great Sources of

[1] D. S. L. Cardwell, *The Organisation of Science in England*, Heinemann, 1957, p. 27.
[2] *Reports of the Late John Smeaton*, 1812, vol. i, pp. ii–vi, quoted in A. M. Carr-Saunders and P. A. Wilson, *The Professions*, O.U.P., 1933, p. 157.
[3] J. H. T. Tudsbury, 'Record of the Origin and Progress of the Institution', *Minutes of the Proceedings of the Institution of Civil Engineers*, vol. ccv (1917–18), Part 1, p. 216, quoted in Carr-Saunders and Wilson, op. cit., p. 157.

Power in Nature for the use and convenience of man'.[1] It was not the more specialized field that it is today, although the major concern then was with roads, bridges, aqueducts and other such works that are now thought of as civil engineering. The Institution retained its emphasis on static engineering while the development and use of machinery was increasing rapidly, and thus failed to satisfy the growing number of engineers with this new and very different interest. Their dissatisfaction was given a focus when the Institution refused to admit George Stephenson as a member unless he filled up a form giving details of his experience, which he would not agree to do,[2] and the incident led in 1847 to the formation of a new body with Stephenson as its first president, the Institution of Mechanical Engineers.

This situation, in which the existing societies fail to cater sufficiently for a new engineering specialism, has recurred many times since. The two other major bodies, the Institution of Naval Architects (founded 1860, Royal 1960) and the Institution of Electrical Engineers (founded 1871), both arose for this reason. The process of fragmentation has continued to the present day, with Institutions for almost all conceivable specialists from Water to Heating and Ventilating, Aeronautical, and Radio Engineers. Apart from these there are also a few small non-specialist bodies, such as the Society of Engineers, the Junior Institution of Engineers, and the Engineers' Guild. The last is a special body whose membership was for some time open only to corporate members of the Institutions of Civil, Mechanical, Electrical and Chemical Engineers, but from 1963 to the members of all bodies which are affiliated to the Joint Engineering Council. It has no study or technical activities and is concerned solely with professional protection.

The position is less complicated amongst the scientific and non-engineering specialist bodies. There was a Chemical Society, a learned body, formed in 1841, and the Institute of Chemistry, much more like a professional association than any of the engineering Institutions, in 1878. Physicists had been academically served by a number of local and specialist study

---

[1] *Charter of the Institution of Civil Engineers*, 1828, quoted in Carr-Saunders and Wilson, op. cit., p. 155.

[2] S. Smiles, *Lives of the Engineers*, 1861, vol. iii, p. 479, quoted in Carr-Saunders and Wilson, op. cit., p. 161.

societies, but it was not until 1920 that the Institute of Physics, a professional body on the lines of that for chemists, was founded. Before this 'the physicist had hardly been recognized as a member of one of the professions'.[1] The Institution of Metallurgists, founded in 1945, is another similar body. Although there had been several technical Institutes, until this Institution was formed 'metallurgists had no professional organization of their own'.[2]

There have also grown up a number of specialist technical bodies other than those for engineers, many of them with an emphasis on practical industrial rather than on academic knowledge, ranging, for example, from Institutes for Iron and Steel to Textiles and Plastics.

## AIMS AND ACTIVITIES

### Study function

In Chapter 2 it was argued that a professional association is primarily concerned with status. There is an emphasis on qualification, bestowed by the association itself or by some educational body, which may be either an indication of competence, or, in a more developed form, a licence to practise. Basically the intention is the same—to guarantee to the prospective client (using the word to include employers) that the practitioner for whose services he is paying does have at least a minimum level of competence. Those bodies, therefore, which do not require any special academic qualification for membership, or nothing beyond evidence of employment in the relevant industrial field, cannot be considered in any real way as professional, and are excluded from this study. In fact this excludes only a few associations although, as will be seen later, many more are commonly denied, and may not even claim, professional status.

Associations with study functions pure and simple are excluded, but it must be remembered that these were the functions for which the earliest bodies were founded, and the emphasis on them has remained to the present day. Its

[1] Institute of Physics, *Objects of the Institute*, 1930, p. 5, quoted in Carr-Saunders and Wilson, op. cit., p. 175.
[2] Institution of Metallurgists, *Year Book 1960–61*, p. 38.

importance may be seen in any of the Constitutions or Statements of Aims.

> 'The objects and purposes for which the Institution is
> hereby constituted are to promote the development of
> Mechanical Engineering and to facilitate the exchange of
> information and ideas thereon.'[1]
> 'To promote, encourage, advance, and co-ordinate the
> study of metallurgy in all its aspects.'[2]
> 'The objects for which the Institute and Society is
> established are the advancement and dissemination of a
> knowledge of physics, pure and applied.'[3]
> 'To promote the general advancement of electrical
> science and engineering and their applications; to facilitate
> the exchange of information on these subjects by means of
> meetings, exhibitions, publications, the establishment of
> libraries.'[4]

The activities of the Associations leave no doubt as to the
importance of this function in practice. Members are able to
benefit not only from the regular national and local meetings
at which papers are read and discussed, and from the learned
publications, but also from the more informal exchanges of
experience and ideas.

*Educational function*

Another way in which this object may be pursued is by the
encouragement of the particular study amongst non-members,
more especially those at school or at any of the higher educational establishments. The most important aspect of this is their
co-operation with such bodies in drawing up syllabuses and
courses, and in providing representatives to sit on the various
governing bodies. These activities may be subsumed under the
more general object of 'promoting the study', but it is specifically stated in some Constitutions,

[1] Institution of Mechanical Engineers, *Royal Charter*, 1961, p. 38.
[2] Institution of Metallurgists, *Memorandum of Association*, 1954, para.
3(a).
[3] Institute of Physics and the Physical Society, *General Information*, 1960,
p. 3.
[4] Institution of Electrical Engineers, *The Institution; Its Objects and Organisation*, 1959, p. 2.

'To co-operate with Universities, other Educational Institutions and public Educational Authorities for the furtherance of Education in Engineering Science or Practice.'[1]

'To promote the better education and training of metallurgists and to encourage those interested in the subject to study metallurgy.'[2]

'To co-operate with Government Departments, Universities, other Educational Institutions and public educational authorities for the furtherance of knowledge of and education in chemical engineering, science or practice.'[3]

*Qualifying function*

Much of this concern with education naturally stems from the Institutions' roles as qualifying bodies. Although they all provide complete or partial exemption to holders of other qualifications, the Institutions' own examinations for membership have become of very great importance, especially to non-graduates and those who have failed to get to university.

This requirement of qualification for membership has existed from the earliest days, as witness the George Stephenson incident. It is interesting, however, that, as in this instance, it was not membership which bestowed a qualification, but a prior qualification which gave evidence of eligibility for membership. Only those of the right standard were thought capable of contributing to and benefiting from the 'exchange of ideas and information'. In these early days, as is to be expected in view of the origins of engineering, the emphasis was very much on practical experience, and it was not until the Institutions began to set entrance examinations that there was a clear shift of emphasis from 'eligibility for membership' to 'qualification by membership'. To be a member of an Institution and to have the right to letters after the name becomes honorific, which means that the Institution, by its previous policy, has gained outside recognition of its select character. For the individual the letters after his name are a proof to his colleagues and present or prospective employer that he has attained a

[1] I.Mech.E., op. cit., para. 7(d).
[2] Institution of Metallurgists, op. cit., para. 3(c).
[3] Institution of Chemical Engineers, *Royal Charter*, 1957, para. 7(d).

given level of competence, in fact a relatively high one. For the employer, provided that he recognizes the status of the Institution, it is a form of guarantee. There are thus three interrelated pressures determining the status accorded to an Institution: the members who try to prove their value, the prospective members, who assess the worth of membership largely in terms of the qualification demanded by employers and others, who are themselves influenced by their opinion of the members and the scarcity or otherwise of the qualification.

The Institute of Chemistry was probably the earliest of the associations to stress the aspect of qualification by membership. Indeed it was founded with qualification as its major function, since the Chemical Society was unable by its Charter to make requirements for membership. There had been a demand for this for some time, but it was with the passing of the Food and Drugs Act in 1875 and the consequent demand for competent public analysts[1] that the need became acute. It was not until 1897 that the first of the engineering Institutions, the I.C.E., began to set entrance examinations, and it was followed by the others, the I.Mech.E. and the I.E.E. in 1912 and 1913 respectively. The qualifying function is explicitly recognized by some of the bodies in their Aims and Objects.

'To act as a qualifying body, conferring membership on those whose qualifications fulfil the requirements of the Bye-Laws of the Institution.'[2]

'To maintain a register of persons qualified as metallurgists by admission to one of the Classes of Membership of the Institution.'[3]

'The Royal Institute of Chemistry is the qualifying professional organization for Chemists.'[4]

There are others however that do not make any specific mention of this function—the I.Mech.E., for example, does not have it as one of its 'objects and purposes'. Even where it is mentioned, as in the Charter of the I.Chem.E., there may be still a strong echo of the eligibility for membership aspect.

[1] See Carr-Saunders and Wilson, op. cit., pp. 167–8.
[2] I.E.E., op. cit., p. 2.      [3] Institution of Metallurgists, op. cit., para. 3(d).
[4] Royal Institute of Chemistry, *Regulations for Admission to Membership*, 1960, p. 1.

'To uphold the status of the Institution by holding or prescribing examinations for candidates for election to Corporate Membership and Non-Corporate Membership and by requiring standards of knowledge and experience approved by the Institution.'[1]

It is, one should note, the status of the Institution which has to be upheld, not the qualifications of the members – although, of course, this will follow.

The letters after the name, however, are not forgotten. The I.Mech.E., which otherwise makes no mention of qualification, provides nevertheless that 'each Member shall be entitled to the use after his name of the initials "M.I.Mech.E."; each Associate Member . . . "A.M.I.Mech.E." ', etc.[2] A similar provision is found in most other Constitutions.

The subjects required for qualification are naturally those largely to do with the particular branch of science or technology with which the association is concerned. There is usually a requirement of proof of a general education at a fairly elementary level, G.C.E. Ordinary level, English Language and Mathematics, for example. The I.Mech.E. are somewhat exceptional in requiring for Associate Membership a knowledge of Industrial Administration, which includes some elementary law, economics and accounting, probably because certain aspects of administration, production engineering for example, are closely allied to mechanical engineering.

Almost all the associations share a basically similar pattern of membership grades. Studentship is for those following a recognized course of study who intend to seek full membership. Graduateship is for those who have passed the Institution's examinations, or have been exempted from them, but who have not yet had sufficient practical experience of a suitably responsible nature. This grade is normally open to holders of university degrees in the relevant subject, as in the I.Mech.E., but it may be limited to those with honours degrees, as in the Institute of Physics. Other degrees and H.N.C. subjects usually give partial exemptions. The intention of nearly all the bodies is to make the entrance requirements for this basic non-corporate grade the equivalent of a university honours degree at least. The R.I.C. claims that in the Graduate Membership Examina-

---

[1] I.Chem.E., op. cit., para. 7(e).  [2] I.Mech.E., op. cit., para. 14.

tion 'the standard of Part 2 . . . is equivalent to that of a good honours degree'.[1]

The first grade of corporate membership, with full voting rights, is normally the Associateship or Associate Membership. There is rarely any further educational requirements beyond that for Graduateship, except for the I.Mech.E., with its insistence on a knowledge of Industrial Administration. Those of Graduate status are admitted to the corporate grade after a sufficient period, usually three years at least, of practical experience in a responsible position. Others may also be admitted direct to the grade if they have the qualifications required for Graduateship together with the necessary practical experience. In rare cases it may also be open to those without the educational qualifications but who are older and have had long practical experience at a high level. Such people may be required to submit a thesis.

The highest grade is that of Member or Fellow, to which an Associate Member may be admitted after further experience. This is a fairly exclusive grade, for senior members of the profession with an 'established reputation'.

*Professional conduct function*

The Institutions all make some explicit reference to their function of controlling the professional conduct of their members. These references however are in very general terms and in most cases could hardly be called an ethical code.

> 'To adopt any lawful means conducive to the setting up and maintenance of a standard of professional conduct amongst metallurgists.'[2]
> 'To promote just and honourable practice in the profession of water engineering, management and administration, and to suppress malpractice.'[3]

Even the regulation of professional conduct may be seen as an aspect of the 'advancement of the science' object, as in the following example.

[1] R.I.C., op. cit., p. 5.
[2] Institution of Metallurgists, op. cit., para. 3(e).
[3] Institution of Water Engineers, *Memorandum of Association*, 1960, para. 3(10).

'In order to facilitate the advancement of the science of mechanical engineering by preserving the respect in which the community holds persons who are engaged in the profession of mechanical engineering, every member shall so order his conduct as to uphold the reputation of the Institution and the dignity of the profession of Mechanical Engineer, and shall, in whatever capacity he may be engaged, act in a strictly fiduciary manner towards clients and employers, towards others with whom his work is connected, and towards other members.'[1]

The ultimate sanction against an erring member is expulsion.

'If any Corporate or Non-Corporate Member shall refuse or wilfully neglect to comply with any of these By-Laws or shall have been guilty of such conduct as in the opinion of the Council either shall have rendered him unfit to remain a member of the Institution or shall be injurious to the Institution, such a member may by a resolution of the Council be expelled from membership. . . . The name and recorded address of a member expelled under this By-Law shall be published in such a manner as the Council may decide.'[2]

The Textile Institute goes further than most of the other associations.

'To define and enforce among members of the Institute strict rules of professional conduct.'[3]

The Institute has drawn up such strict rules in its 'Professional Code of Practice'. This refers, however, only to those 'acting professionally in a consultative capacity'.[4] The I.C.E. also has a code of practice, but this again applies only to consultants, a small minority even amongst civil engineers. In practice, for all but consultants, there are few rules of conduct that the Institutions could lay down that would not already be covered by the law or an employer's contract, and these are in no way specifically professional. Since there are few, if any rules, there can be few, or no transgressions. A serious crime would

[1] I.Mech.E., op. cit., By-law 34.
[2] Ibid., By-law 35.
[3] Textile Institute, *Royal Charter*, 1956, para. 2(g).
[4] Textile Institute, *Professional Code of Conduct*, 1958, p. 3.

probably make a member liable to expulsion, but this is very rare. Regulation of professional conduct for the great majority of members, therefore, can hardly be said to exist.

*Protective function*

Many of the associations, particularly the engineering Institutions, see the above functions as the limit of their activities. The great emphasis that they place on the study function may make it appear that these bodies are not professional at all in the way that the R.I.B.A. or the B.M.A. are. Although, as in the case of the I.Mech.E., there may be no specific mention of qualification this is the most important function of such bodies as far as professionalism is concerned. They are not prepared to pursue the question of status further than this, except, when the body has obtained a Royal Charter, in securing for their members a monopoly of the term 'Chartered Mechanical Engineer',[1] 'Chartered Textile Technologist',[2] etc. This reluctance to undertake any of the protective functions which are normally associated with a professional body may appear strange, even more so when it is remembered that some of the major Institutions, those to whom professional status is most readily granted, are amongst those most careful to limit themselves in this way.

In part this is traditional. The primary object of most of these associations, as has been seen, was and is to further the study of the particular science or technology. The qualifying function is only secondary to this, and was in fact only undertaken at a fairly late date. It was then thought necessary just to uphold the value of the qualification, and little more. Before the First World War the I.C.E. made it clear that although it 'attempted to ensure that those appointed to engineering posts (in the public services) shall have at least the qualifications which are demanded from associates of the Institution . . . this, however, does not mean that the Institution is prepared to take much interest in matters of salary'.[3] Somewhat later, at the 1926 annual meeting of the I.Mech.E., 'a member inquired what the Institution was doing "to improve the status of the mechanical

---

[1] I.Mech.E., op. cit., para. 17.
[2] Textile Institute, *Royal Charter (Supplemental)*, 1956, para. 9.
[3] Carr-Saunders and Wilson, op. cit., p. 163.

engineer". This unexpected intervention seems to have been very coldly received.'[1] In their Royal Charters the Institutions have limited themselves more definitely. As the I.E.E. says: 'It will be seen from the terms of the Royal Charter that the Institution, being constituted to promote the general advancement of science, cannot act in matters touching the personal gain of individual members, and it has been made clear by the Council that they have no wish for this position, in which lies much of the Institution's strength, to be altered.'[2] This is undoubtedly a widely felt sentiment. More recently the limitation has been reinforced by the requirements of the Inland Revenue respecting technical and study societies, so that for financial reasons the Institutions are now very wary of doing anything more, even if they wanted, than they are strictly allowed.

Other associations, however, certainly undertake the protective function, and say so explicitly in their literature.

> 'To promote in every possible way the interests of and to maintain and enhance the status and prestige of metallurgists.'[3]

Similarly one of the objects of the Institute of Physics is 'the elevation of the profession of physics',[4] while one of the 'main concerns' of the R.I.C. is 'to look after the professional interests of chemists'.[5]

The more important of these bodies were in fact founded with this as one of their major objects. The R.I.C. was formed as a qualifying body, but also with the protective function in mind, since there was, among the younger practitioners at the time, 'a long pent-up feeling of dissatisfaction at the deficiency of means for exerting a common action and influence'.[6] The Institute of Physics, similarly, was formed on the initiative of the Council of the Physical Society, among other things 'to improve the professional status of physicists'.[7] Again, the Insti-

---

[1] Ibid., p. 161.   [2] I.E.E., op. cit., p. 3.
[3] Institution of Metallurgists, op. cit., p. 3.
[4] Institute of Physics, etc., *Membership Regulations*, 1961, p. 3.
[5] R.I.C., *Looking to Chemistry for a Career*, 1959.
[6] Professor Odling, Institute of Chemistry, *Jubilee Celebrations*, 1928, quoted in Carr-Saunders and Wilson, op. cit., p. 169.
[7] Institute of Physics, etc., *General Information*, 1960, p. 3.

tution of Metallurgists, 'having functions independent of, but supplementary to those of the Iron and Steel Institute and the Institute of Metals', was founded with the 'help and goodwill' of these Institutes, so that 'by joining forces in this way metallurgists are reaching a far stronger position to promote the welfare of the profession, to improve and maintain its standing, and to secure its adequate recognition'.[1]

Although mainly founded for the qualifying and protective functions, all three of these bodies have nevertheless shown an interesting tendency to increase their study activities. In the case of the R.I.C. Carr-Saunders and Wilson noted that the 'pent-up feeling of dissatisfaction' mentioned above 'has not been entirely dispelled'.[2] They attributed this to the limits placed on the Institute's activities–'The Institute can attract and hold members neither by study facilities nor by trade-union activities, but only by the prestige which may appertain to the letters A.I.C. and F.I.C'.[3] More will be said about trade unionism later, but as regards study facilities there does seem to have been an expansion since the last war. Meetings in London and at a number of local branches are held to hear lectures and discuss papers, and reflecting this greater activity there has been 'a notable expansion of the Journal . . . in the late 1940's with its natural sequel in the decision to double the frequency of publication, which took effect in 1953'.[4] Also, with an increase in the numbers of students studying chemistry outside the universities, the importance of the Institute's qualifying examinations and letters (now) A.R.I.C. and F.R.I.C. have risen.

The Institute of Physics has co-operated with the Physical Society from the beginning, with the broad principle that the latter should concern itself with pure physics and the former with its applications. However, since it became increasingly difficult to draw the distinction, the two bodies were amalgamated in 1960. The same process may be at work in the Institution of Metallurgists. Its study activities are not extensive, as these are mostly left to the technical bodies, but a scheme of joint subscription has now been devised, and this may pave the

[1] Institution of Metallurgists, *Year Book 1960–61*, p. 38.

[2] Carr-Saunders and Wilson, op. cit., p. 169.

[3] Ibid., p. 169.

[4] R.I.C., Report of the Council (1959), *Journal*, 1959, vol. 83, supplement p. 17.

way to closer co-operation and perhaps eventually amalgamation.

The majority of the smaller engineering bodies have followed the example of the major Institutions in limiting their protective activities. Although the Institution of Production Engineers, for example, was formed among other things in order to 'establish the status and designation of a production or manufacturing engineer',[1] it shows more a desire to define a new field of study and to identify its practitioners than a concern with social status. The small Society of Engineers has as one of its objects 'to watch over and protect the interest of persons engaged in the engineering profession',[2] but its activities in this field seem to be negligible. Some other bodies do a little more. The Institution of Water Engineers has as one object 'to watch over and promote the interest of the members',[3] whilst the Institution of Engineering Designers aims 'to raise the professional status of the more responsible Engineering Draughtsmen and particularly of Engineering Designers'.[4]

As far as the protective function is concerned the most important body for engineers is the Engineers' Guild. It was founded in 1938, having as its objects 'to promote and maintain the unity, public usefulness, honour and interests of the engineering profession – broadly speaking, to do for professional engineers the sort of thing that the B.M.A. does for doctors'.[5] This comparison with other professions is frequently made. One leaflet begins – 'It is a galling fact that the professional engineer lacks the prestige of medical, legal and architectural colleagues. Why? The reason is simple. These professions are guarded by powerful protective organizations sustained by large membership. The majority of professional engineers, by contrast, are astonishingly apathetic to the need for united representation at a time when only the united voice commands attention.'[6]

The existence of the Engineers' Guild is an implicit recognition of the limited powers of the Institutions. These 'are

---

[1] Institution of Production Engineers, *Notes on the History and Activities of the Institution*, 1958, p. 2.

[2] Society of Engineers (Inc.), *Memorandum of Association*, 1958, para. 3(2).

[3] I.W.E., op. cit., para. 3(12).

[4] Institution of Engineering Designers, *General Information*, 1960, p. 3.

[5] Engineers' Guild, *An Introduction to its Aims and Achievements*, 1959.

[6] Engineers' Guild, *Face Facts*, 1952.

"learned societies", dedicated to the advancement of engineering—not the advancement of engineers. This is completely omitted from their Charters.' 'They accept the need for a separate body to handle those matters with which they cannot deal', and they have formed with the Guild a Joint Consultative Committee 'for the regular exchange of views on questions affecting the profession'. Many members of the Councils of the Institutions are members of the Guild, and there are usually several on the Guild Council. The engineering profession is thought to need an association 'because without it neither government, nor employers, nor the public at large understands the needs of the profession. Trained and qualified men are confused with machine-minders or dismissed as "back-room boys" by the general public. Individual engineers have no authoritative support from their profession in disputes about conditions of employment.'[1]

A concern with the protection and raising of status does not explain what is done in practice to attain this object. It must be borne in mind from the outset that the associations are not free to do whatever they wish in this respect. Since they are all incorporated under the Companies Acts, they are precluded from trade-union activities. In the 'Articles of Association' of all but the purely learned societies, where there is no doubt about their functions, there is a standard clause that the Institution 'shall not support with its funds any object, or endeavour to impose on or procure to be observed by its members or others any regulation, restriction or condition, which, if an object of the [Institution] would make it a trade union'. This means that they have very limited powers to deal directly with salaries or conditions of employment. The legal position of these bodies was made clear in the case of Jenkin v. The Pharmaceutical Society, by which the latter was prescribed from performing the functions of an employers' association. The principle applies equally to bodies acting as trade unions, and the case certainly crystallized the attitude of the Institute of Chemistry.[2]

The associations can and do attempt to deal with salaries indirectly. Four of them, the R.I.C., the Institute of Physics, the Institution of Metallurgists and the Engineers' Guild,

---

[1] Engineers' Guild, *An Introduction . . .*, 1959.
[2] See Carr-Saunders and Wilson, op. cit., p. 169.

conduct periodic salary surveys. The R.I.C. was the first to do so in 1930, since when it has carried out a further seven, with the latest in 1962. The Institute of Physics and the Institution of Metallurgists began in 1948, and have held another five and three surveys respectively since then, with the latest in 1960 and 1963. The Engineers' Guild made its first survey in 1956, undertaken jointly with the Royal Commission on Doctors' and Dentists' Remuneration, and it has followed this with others in 1960 and 1963. They all gather information on age, occupation and grade of membership for correlation with salary.

Except in the case of the Guild it is emphasized that the surveys are purely factual statements.

'It was thought desirable to preserve the strict objectivity of the survey by avoiding the introduction of inferences or conclusions based on external evidence' (i.e. cost-of-living indexes). 'Any attempt to establish either standard or minimum salaries for individual chemists or groups depending solely on age, qualifications and length of employment, would not take into account the value of personal qualities on which the suitability of a professional man for posts of senior responsibility must depend.'[1]

'The Report is not a guide to the salaries appropriate to all graduates in physics: much less is it a scale or set of scales recommended by the Council of the Institute of Physics and the Physical Society. The Report is a factual summary of the emoluments received by members of certain grades of the Institute of Physics and, since there is a clear difference between the average incomes of members of the same age in the different grades, due regard must be paid to the qualifications implied by these gradings.'[2]

'The Institution's remuneration surveys are not intended to provide simple substitutes for age-graded salary scales for metallurgists; they aim at giving a factual record of the remuneration of that proportion of the Institution's members who take part.'[3]

The Engineers' Guild is less wary about the use to which the results of its survey are put. It is much more frank about their value, to both employers and employees. They 'can now see

[1] R.I.C., op. cit., p. 14.　　[2] Institute of Physics, etc., *Salary Survey*, 1960, p. 1.
[3] Institution of Metallurgists, *Remuneration Survey*, 1960.

how particular salaries stand in relation to the general level.
Both are likely to claim that the jobs they are concerned with
deserve at least an average degree of competence on the one
hand, and of reward on the other.' 'Past, present and future
surveys will be a continuing influence in raising unjustifiably
low salaries. Some jobs may be found not to bear the increase,
and the general answer will be that these ought not to be held
by qualified engineers at all.'[1] The value, then, is seen to be
twofold; making members aware of average salaries, so that the
lower-paid ones are provided with an argument for levelling
upward, and ensuring that qualified engineers are not employed
in low paid positions in which their skill is not fully utilized.
Equally, it may be of value to employers to know the average
rates which are paid for engineers in various circumstances. It
may also evoke outside sympathy and support. 'There was no
doubt that the results of the first survey, which showed engineering to be so ill-rewarded in comparison with other professions, astonished many laymen.'[2]

The Institute of Physics lays more stress on the value of the
surveys to employers than to employees. 'The reports of these
surveys have been widely requested, and apparently valued, by
industrial employers, Government departments, public authorities and others concerned with the salaries of scientists.'[3]
How far beyond this the associations go in the use of their
surveys is difficult to say. They may be willing to give advice
on the proper salary for particular circumstances to employers
who ask for it, as does the Engineers' Guild, or, as in the case of
the Institution of Metallurgists, they may refuse to do even this.
The R.I.C. is to some extent prepared to take the initiative in
matters of salary: 'The Institute can sometimes exert its influence effectively in an advisory capacity, either directly with
employing organizations or indirectly through co-operation
with bodies representing the staff side in established negotiating
machinery. Thus informal discussions on grading, salary scales
and other conditions of service were held during the year with
representatives of certain public authorities and nationalized
industries, as well as with many private employers.'[4]

There are, in some circumstances, pressures towards trade-

[1] Engineers' Guild, 'The Effect of Knowing', *The Professional Engineer*,
vol. 6, no. 9, Jan. 1961, p. 327.          [2] Ibid., p. 327.
[3] Institute of Physics, etc., op. cit., p. 1.     [4] R.I.C., op. cit., p. 14.

union, collective bargaining activities, even though the particular body may not take much general interest in salary problems. Two specialist engineering bodies, the Institution of Water Engineers and the Institution of Hospital Engineers, are included in the Ministry of Labour's Index of trade unions. Both have members who are almost wholly employed in public bodies, and it is of interest that the favourable climate towards collective bargaining in these has influenced the activities of these essentially learned societies. The first of the two bodies was the only association to which nearly all the high-ranking engineers in water undertakings belonged, and so it was prevailed upon to represent them. The Institution of Municipal Engineers was at one time in a somewhat similar situation and paid a good deal of attention to salaries, until it obtained a Royal Charter and left activities of this kind to the local government trade unions.[1]

The Engineers' Guild does not engage at all in collective bargaining. This is partly because of a certain antipathy towards trade unionism amongst a part of the membership, but is also due to lack of opportunity. The fields in which it has the greatest representation (mostly public authorities) are those in which other organizations for the purpose already exist. In fact even where it does have relatively strong representation its further growth is hindered by these other bodies, which have a much clearer function. The Guild itself is not completely antipathetic, however, since it did once try to take the opportunity of becoming the only body to represent engineers in a newly-nationalized industry, Iron and Steel. It 'requested the Ministry of Supply to recognize the Guild as the appropriate organization to represent the interests of Chartered Civil, Mechanical and Electrical Engineers who were to be employed in the staffs under the general direction of the Iron and Steel Corporation of Great Britain'. In the end there was no central negotiating machinery set up, but the Guild concluded that this 'indicates the need for Guild Branches to undertake local responsibility for Guild work', and proposed intensive and extensive recruitment in the industry.[2] It also tried to secure

[1] See Carr-Saunders and Wilson, op. cit., p. 159, for an example of its earlier activities.
[2] Engineers' Guild, *Journal of the Engineers' Guild*, vol. 2, no. 2, March 1951, p. 40.

recognition from the London Transport Executive as the appropriate body for qualified engineers, but was told that the existing machinery was adequate. The Guild pointed the moral of this to its members, that 'this attitude can only be expected until the Guild can claim to represent a majority of the engineers concerned'.[1]

More recently the Guild has adopted a more definite attitude against collective bargaining in a report prepared by its Professional Interests Sub-Committee. After discussing the pros and cons of collective bargaining the report concludes that this is 'inconsistent with the professional standing of the engineer and with his proper relationship towards his employer', and that it creates 'a threat to the future status of professional engineers, both individually and collectively, serious enough to require action on behalf of the profession'. The action they suggested was 'to secure acceptance as the recognized consultant to engineers and their employers on the interests of the profession', 'to seek legislation enabling professional engineers to withdraw, as a group, from collective bargaining machinery', and 'to influence the activities of joint negotiating committees in so far as matters of professional concern are involved'.[2]

Most of its present efforts in this direction are aimed much more at trying to persuade employers to require proper qualifications (i.e. membership of one of the major Institutions), and to offer suitable salaries when advertising a post. This activity is mostly directed at public bodies, with whom it also tries to insist that engineers are not employed in positions of lower status than other professionals. It has had some disputes with local authorities who have attempted to make trade-union membership a condition of employment. As the Guild says of itself, it 'applies pressure to employers who seek to impose unacceptable conditions of service, and helps in cases of wrongful dismissal or termination without adequate compensation'. It also 'gives . . . advice on the interpretation of service agreements, contracts, and other legal matters', and 'has helped more than 200 members during the last three years alone with professional problems'. The aims of the Guild are shown by the activities which it would like to undertake if it had more adequate representation, which are to 'consult increasingly with

[1] Engineers' Guild, *Journal*, vol. 2, no. 6, Nov. 1951, p. 167.
[2] Engineers' Guild, *Collective Bargaining*, 1959.

Government departments and other official bodies on professional problems', to 'establish standards of remuneration and conditions of service appropriate to the various levels of professional responsibility', and to 'co-operate with other associations in seeking material improvements in the relative financial position of the professional classes'.[1]

Some of the other associations also give advice to individual members, though they are limited in how far they can go. The R.I.C. points out that 'although the officers are able to give information on matters of principle and to explain the customary procedure for meeting a particular situation, they cannot normally undertake to intervene in any dispute'.[2] The Institute of Physics is similarly prepared to give individual advice, stating that 'a good deal of the professional work of the Institute concerns members' personal queries about such matters as contracts of service, consulting fees, changes of posts, and so forth', but that 'it cannot negotiate on behalf of its members on remuneration'.[3]

Those organizations, among them the Institution of Metallurgists and the Engineers' Guild, which have an appointments register, try to use it to protect their members' interests by restricting the posts advertised to those of which they approve, and by circulating them only to their members. Unfortunately, these registers are never very satisfactory, for various reasons, and are not greatly used.

Other bodies, which do not undertake any of the protective functions discussed above, sometimes include in their constitutions a standard clause about legal and professional aid. It is found, for example, with the Institutions of Water Engineers and of Highway Engineers.

> 'To provide legal or other professional assistance for the protection of the interests of any Member or Members of the water [highway] engineering profession in cases which may be deemed to involve questions of principle affecting the profession generally and not the individual interests of the parties litigating only.'[4]

[1] Engineers' Guild, *An Introduction* . . ., 1959.
[2] R.I.C., op. cit., p. 14.
[3] Institute of Physics, etc., *General Information*, 1960, p. 8.
[4] I.W.E., op. cit., para. 3(13); Institution of Highway Engineers, *Memorandum*, para. 3(5).

PROFESSIONAL ASSOCIATIONS

## Conclusion

To sum up the aims and activities of the professional associations for scientists and engineers, it is clear that the major emphasis is on the study function. This is true not only of the engineering Institutions, of which there is one for almost every specialism of any importance, but even of those other Institutes which were founded primarily to perform other functions than that of study. A purely study or learned society cannot be a professional body, but the function which makes it one, that of qualification, only arises out of the study function. Qualification by these bodies in no case carries with it a monopoly of practice, as it does for example in medicine. It is solely a hallmark of competence. Membership usually implies the acceptance of a code of conduct, but for those who are salaried employees, that is, the great majority, this code means little or nothing more than what is required of them anyway as employees. The threat of dismissal is more real than the threat of expulsion from the association. Having taken an individual into membership many of the Institutions see little more that they can do for him, other than to guard against any lowering of the entrance standards. Other associations carry out more protective activities and are therefore more clearly professional than the learned societies. In the case of the senior engineering Institutions their somewhat ambiguous nature has resulted, with their encouragement, in the formation of a separate professional association, to which, however, only a small proportion of professional engineers belong.

This chapter has not attempted to ascribe professional status to some groups or to withhold it from others. Instead it has taken a number of bodies whose members claim to be professional people and described their activities. As was argued in the second chapter, the main consideration is not the details of the organization of a particular group but the fact that they want and claim to be professionals. It is their attitudes which will determine their behaviour, rather than other people's opinions of whether or not they are 'a profession'. Of course such opinions may affect their own attitudes, but equally their behaviour will influence the judgements of others. It is therefore to the attitudes of these professionals that the study now proceeds.

# CHAPTER FIVE

# Professional People – 1

---

## THE INSTITUTION OF METALLURGISTS

The Institution of Metallurgists has already been mentioned several times in the previous chapter. As was seen there it is in most respects typical, though naturally it has individual characteristics. It was founded in 1945 as a professional body complementary to the two main existing technical bodies. This makes it different from the major engineering Institutions, which are mostly learned bodies themselves, but more like the associations for chemists and physicists. This is an advantage, since it is useful to have a reasonably clear distinction between the technical and professional functions when a special study of the latter is being made. Metallurgists are not a very numerous group, and the Institution is therefore fairly small, with a membership of just over 4,400 in 1961. In terms of the last chapter its main functions are education – the encouragement of the study of metallurgy and the provision of facilities for students; qualification; and protection – by means of regular salary surveys and an appointments register. Its study function is limited because of the existence of other bodies, but it does hold refresher courses on particular topics, and prints articles of general metallurgical interest in its journal.

The information on which this chapter is based is derived from a postal questionnaire sent to a 10 per cent sample of all Fellows, Associates, Licentiates and Students of the Institution. There were 286 usable questionnaires returned, a net response rate of 67 per cent. Further details of the survey and the methods used are given in the Appendix.

## EDUCATIONAL AND WORK BACKGROUND

Some idea of the sort of people with whom this chapter deals can be gained from a consideration of their backgrounds, particularly the education they have had and the work they now do. The educational background of the respondents not only shows the patterns of education followed by entrants to the profession, but gives also an indication of their social origins. Taking together the three corporate grades (Fellows, Associates and Licentiates), those who went to grammar school and followed this with only part-time higher education were by far the most numerous group, comprising 44 per cent of the total. If one adds those who attended elementary and non-grammar secondary schools (7 per cent) and public schools (4 per cent) with part-time higher education, the proportion whose full-time education finished at school rises to 55 per cent. Only a small proportion (10·5 per cent) attended technical college on a full-time basis, but one-third of the total sample went to university, mostly from grammar school, and this was the second most popular route to qualification.

When the three grades are compared it is clear that graduates are most likely to reach the grade of Fellow, the top of the profession. Graduates constitute three-fifths of the Fellows, but only one-third of Associates and one-tenth of Licentiates. This is not related to age as there are no significant variations in educational patterns with age. When the group of Fellows born in 1910–19 is compared with the same group of Associates, there are only 7 graduates in the latter 20 as against 14 in the former 20. The small proportion amongst the Licentiates is probably due to the fact that most graduates wait until they have had the necessary practical experience, when they can be elected directly into the Associate grade. There is a similar, but less marked tendency for those from public schools to advance more easily to Fellowship–there are 20 per cent of them in this grade compared with only 8 per cent in each of the other two.

The total proportion from public schools is, in fact, quite large (11 per cent), and this group, together with those who attended university, are likely to come from a fairly high social background. This seems a reasonable assumption in view of the lengthy training involved and the known facts about the influence of social class on educational attainment, especially at the higher levels.[1]

There remain, however, the 55 per cent whose higher education was only part-time, who might well have lower social origins. Most went to grammar schools, but of course these, too, are open to the same social class influences which tend to discriminate against the working class, first at the eleven-plus examination, then at the leaving age of 15 and again after 'O' level G.C.E. Therefore the age at which full-time education ends can be taken as a good indication of social background.

Of those with part-time higher education, only a few left at 15, but substantially more did so at 16. Together they make up over half the total, which suggests that many entrants to the profession have come from social strata below the one to which they have attained. With the great expansion of this type of work this is to be expected. Part-time education does seem to some extent to provide an avenue of upward mobility parallel to full-time education for those who cannot take advantage of the latter, but, as has been pointed out, these are not the individuals most likely to advance in the profession. Taken as a whole, then, the evidence from the present sample suggests that the majority have been recruited from the higher social strata.

The great majority of metallurgists (76 per cent) are employed in private industry. There are smaller numbers (about 9 per cent each) employed in nationalized industry and engaged in Education. A few more are employed by the government or are self-employed. As to the type of work that they do, nearly one-quarter of all respondents are in management positions, and just slightly more are engaged in research and development. The proportions vary considerably between grades, so that whilst there are 51 per cent of Fellows in management, there are only 22 per cent of Associates and 14 per cent of Licentiates. This does not appear to be wholly a factor of age, since, for example, there is a great difference between Fellows born 1910–19 when compared with the same group of Associates. To be more precise, 55 per cent of the former are in management, but only 12·5 per cent of the latter.

[1] The most recent presentation of these is to be found in the Robbins' Report. Committee on Higher Education, *Higher Education*, Cmnd. 2154, H.M.S.O., 1963, Report Chapter VI and Appendix One.

Age does have some influence, but only up to around 40 years, after which the proportions in management remain steady. What is clear is that there is a higher proportion of Fellows doing administrative work, which means either that Fellows are more likely to be promoted to such posts or, as is more probable, that members in these positions are more likely to be made Fellows. In other words it is the level reached in his employment, determined by the judgements of his employers rather than by those of his peers, which determines an individual's standing within the profession. It also means that administrative jobs, which may have no direct relationship with the individual's technical skills, are the ones most highly regarded. The criterion of a successful career has little to do with the professional skill, and much more with the typical middle-class employee's conception of success as promotion within the management hierarchy.

It is interesting to see how far educational background is important in determining success in the career, that is, in reaching a management position. Rather surprisingly, graduates do not seem to be particularly favoured, except for those who also went to a public school, by itself easily the most advantageous background. Ex-grammar-school graduates, amongst both Fellows and Associates, seem to do less well than the grammar-school–part-time technical college group, whose chances are twice as good in both grades. When qualifications, rather than educational background, are considered, a similar pattern is found. Those with first and higher degrees are certainly not favoured, and if anything do less well in reaching management posts than those with a diploma.

Educational background and qualifications also have a clear influence on the administrative and technical content of the work performed. This is obviously related to the type of job— managerial work being mostly administrative, research mostly technical, and so on, but when looked at in this way there is a rather different relationship between education and the nature of the work. An analysis of the work content by educational background gives a confusing picture, but this becomes much clearer if qualifications only are considered. There is then a tendency for the higher qualifications to be related to greater administrative content, with the exception of those with higher degrees. The latter, no doubt, are those with a greater liking

86

and aptitude for their subject, who prefer it to other types of work which may be more highly paid. Also they are the individuals who will be most valued, in non-monetary terms, for their technical skill and know-how, and who are likely to be kept in technical work not only because of this, but also because they are probably considered too specialized and too narrowly-trained to be suitable for a position in management.

For the rest, however, it would seem that longer technical training does not serve, except in the short run, to enable individuals to perform the most technically demanding work. On the contrary, its main effect, as with most non-technical qualifications, is to facilitate promotion to largely administrative, managerial jobs, in which only a very little of the technical knowledge gained may be used.

## ATTITUDES TOWARDS THE INSTITUTION

Having looked at the educational and work background of the members of the Institution, and bearing in mind the officially-defined functions of this and other professional bodies as described in the previous chapter, the next step is to describe the attitudes of members towards the Institution—why they have joined it, what they see as its functions, what activities they think it ought to undertake, and which of its services they make use of.

### TABLE 1
#### Reason for Joining the Institution

| | |
|---|---|
| Qualification | 154 |
| Need for Professional Body | 32 |
| Support Standards | 12 |
| Publications | 11 |
| Raise Status | 11 |
| Keep in Contact | 10 |
| Other | 14 |
| N.A. | 1 |
| Total | 246 |

First of all, why have its members joined the Institution? Table 1 shows that, taking all members together, over 62 per cent joined in order to get a qualification for themselves, that is, for the sake of the letters after their name. 'To obtain a qualification' was the most common answer to this question, but some respondents were more explicit, the following for example, who show the different needs of the more and less qualified.

> 'After nearly forty years of hard work and substantial achievement it seemed a good way of making everyone aware of the fact and establishing a certain known level of achievement in my subject.' (Fellow)

> 'To obtain a professional qualification in metallurgy and thus to further my status as a metallurgist.' (Associate)

> 'As an additional qualification as a metallurgist particularly should I wish to change my job.' (Associate)

> 'To obtain professional qualifications and thereby qualify for increased remunerations and also for future use in case of change of employment.' (Licentiate)

Only occasionally is it stated explicitly that the qualification was needed for personal advancement, but this is really implicit in most. It is noticeable that this response is given much less by Fellows, and rather more by Licentiates than by Associates. This is understandable when it is remembered that the Institution was quite recently founded, so that many of the present Fellows will have entered directly into this grade. They would already have attained to the higher positions in their work and would thus be less likely to need an extra qualification for advancement. Even if the Institution were older and the Fellows had worked their way up from the lower grades, there might still be a similar tendency. Although the question asked was the reason for joining at the time of doing so, their answer can, in fact, only relate to what they now think was their reason. Age and experience could well alter this from a more egocentric reason of getting a qualification to something more 'idealistic'. Ignoring the factor of grades, there is certainly an increasing emphasis on qualification amongst the younger age-groups. Nevertheless, this egocentric reason for joining is still one of the most frequently given by Fellows and is by far the most important for the other two grades. The somewhat greater frequency of this reply amongst Licentiates is probably a result of the factors just discussed and partly of the fact that there are far fewer graduates, who are less likely to need more qualifications, in this grade. However, it should not be assumed that graduates do not need the extra qualification at all, since two-thirds give this as their reason for joining.

Other reasons came far behind that of obtaining a qualification. The next most frequent is the recognition of the need for a professional body, which is given by 13 per cent of all members. Amongst Fellows it is as important as qualification, but Associates mention it much less and Licentiates hardly at all. It is rather a vague response, somewhat 'idealistic' (which probably accounts for its popularity with Fellows) and is intended to encompass everything that the individual thinks of as being a function of a professional body – to confer qualifications, protect professional status, encourage the study of the subject and so on.

The following examples are typical.

> 'After all this is the official body of my chosen profession.'
> 'To subscribe to the first recognized body ever set up purely for metallurgists as such.'
> 'Because I agreed on the desirability of forming a Professional Body for the Metallurgical Profession.'

Some of these particular aspects are mentioned specifically in the other responses. Thus 'helping to support educational standards' and 'helping to raise professional status' are each given by about 5 per cent of respondents, more often by Fellows than Associates, and not at all by Licentiates. Rather more of the latter say that they joined in order to receive the Institution's publications, that is the Journal and other occasional reports – in fact it is the second most popular response of this group. The obvious reason is that many of them joined when they were students and so in need of the technical literature. The argument is borne out by the responses of the Students themselves (as a non-corporate grade they are not otherwise dealt with in this chapter) of whom 42 per cent, the largest group, gave this as their reason for joining.

These results tend to confirm the belief that the Institution is regarded mainly as a body which sets examinations and bestows qualifications, a sort of substitute for or, for graduates, a complement to a university, with a few other peripheral functions. As one member stated, rather bitterly, but perhaps voicing the feelings of many non-graduates, 'they confer a limited professional status upon those persons who are denied, by a margin of a few examination marks, the entrance to a University. For this meagre service they extract a membership fee each year, whereas the University bestows an even greater accolade to its successful students–and charges nothing for it.'

It can be argued of course that the reasons why the members originally joined the Institution may not reflect their opinion of its activities and functions which they now consider important. However, the results show that the prime emphasis is still on the Institution's function as a qualifying body. Nearly a half of the total responses (48 per cent) stress the function of the Institution in bestowing qualifications and maintaining examination standards, and in this there is little variation between grades. Undoubtedly, major importance is attached to the qualifying function by the members.

More than one-fifth of the answers suggest that the main function of the Institution is raising or maintaining the status of metallurgists. This response is rather vague, and gives no clue as to what actual methods or activities are thought necessary. Some other responses are more definite about what should be done, but these are very few. They include such things as 'dealing with financial rewards', either directly or by using the Appointments Register, 'stressing the value of the qualification given by the Institution', 'dealing with professional matters', 'more and better public relations' and 'representing metallurgists to government departments, employers and so on'. Taken together, however, these account for less than 10 per cent of the total responses. Even fewer mention 'the provision of technical services', and this is obviously not considered an important function of the Institution, mainly because this is dealt with by the technical Institutes. Even so, this response was given by 12 per cent of Licentiates, the group most concerned with educational publications.

It is also interesting to see which of the Institution's services the members do, in fact, make use of, and this is shown in Table 2. Quite a large minority (17 per cent) did not make use of any, but amongst those who did, the largest number, over 35 per cent, mention publications. A further 12 per cent made use of the Refresher Courses, so that despite the rather unimportant place given to the provision of technical services as a

### TABLE 2

*Services Used*

| | Fellows | Assocs. | Licents. | Total* |
|---|---|---|---|---|
| Publications | 14 | 59 | 48 | 121 |
| Salary Surveys | 6 | 36 | 12 | 54 |
| Refresher Courses | 10 | 27 | 3 | 40 |
| Appointments Register | 3 | 21 | 10 | 34 |
| Educational | 6 | 6 | 4 | 16 |
| Meetings | 1 | 4 | 1 | 6 |
| Publicity | 2 | — | — | 2 |
| All | 1 | 5 | — | 6 |
| Other | — | 1 | — | 1 |
| None | 16 | 27 | 15 | 58 |
| N.A. | 2 | 1 | — | 3 |

\* There were a number of multiple responses.

function of the Institution these are in fact the services most used. There need be no contradiction in this—it means that the services which are directly provided are less important to the members than those activities of the Institution which only affect them indirectly.

The only other sizeable response is that of the 16 per cent who found the salary surveys of use. Since many others may include these with publications it would seem that the services associated with the protective function are welcomed by a proportion of the members.

Fellows tend to use the various services less than the other grades, but they give markedly lower responses mentioning the salary surveys or the Appointments Register, probably because, as successful men, they have no need of them. There are few great differences between Associates and Licentiates, except that far fewer of the latter have used the Refresher Courses. Again this is not surprising, since, being still young, they do not really need refreshing. They also tend to mention the salary surveys a little less, and publications a little more, reflecting probably a concern with getting qualifications and thus, they hope, advancement, rather than with their present salary.

The views of the members on the function of the Institution and their use of the services that it provides have been considered, but what of the functions that they think it ought to perform, or the activities which it ought to carry out but does not?

The responses given provide no evidence of any great dissatisfaction with the Institution or unfulfilled demands for further
activities. Nearly 39 per cent have no ideas for further activities
or suggest only minor ones. There are more suggestions from
Associates than from Fellows or Licentiates, probably because
the former are more satisfied and the latter less willing to imply
criticism of a body which they are likely to have joined only
recently.

Of those who make suggestions, the largest number want
more local meetings. To some extent this reflects a dissatisfaction with the undue centralization on London, but it is also
an indication of a desire for more technical activities, since this
would be the purpose of the meetings. This concern with the
study of metallurgy and the desire that the Institution should
do more to further it also come out in the other major responses. One of these is a demand that there should be more
technical publications, another calls for more co-ordination
with the other metallurgical bodies, which are purely learned
societies, and a third asks for more educational work. None of
these responses is given as often by Fellows, because technical
activities are by now of less value to them, but are much more
popular with Licentiates, who are naturally more involved in
learning and using metallurgical knowledge.

There would seem to be little doubt that it is the technical,
study function which the members would like to see streng-
thened by further activities, even though it is already the technical
services which are amongst the most useful. These demands
show very clearly the importance that members attach to the
study function in their professional body, even when the
technical institutes also exist. Certainly any moves towards
greater co-ordination or even amalgamation would be greatly
welcomed. Without such moves the Institution itself would
probably have to expand its technical activities.

## WORK AND THE INSTITUTION

The aim of this final section is twofold. Firstly, it is to show
how far metallurgists are satisfied with four aspects of the work
that they do—the use made of their professional knowledge and
skill, their status, their opportunities for promotion and their
salary. Secondly, bearing in mind the fact that the members

do not see the Institution as a body much concerned with their conditions of employment, the aim is to see how much more they would like the Institution to do about these matters. In order to avoid the ambiguity which could arise in a postal questionnaire, the question was split into two parts to achieve comparisons within and outside the profession. This makes a response easier for the person who, for example, is quite happy with his own position *vis-à-vis* other metallurgists, but thinks that metallurgists as a whole are poorly treated. The exact reference groups chosen by individuals cannot be known, especially in the case of the out-group, to which the individual could consider himself equal, superior, or inferior, and express his satisfaction with the actual situation accordingly. However, this is not likely to be a serious weakness, since it is the satisfaction recorded rather than the reference group chosen which is important.

Satisfaction with each of the four areas of work is shown in Table 3. Considering first of all the use made of his professional

## TABLE 3
### *Satisfaction with Use Made of Skill, Status, Prospects for Promotion and Salary*

| Compared with: | Skill | Status | Promotion | Salary |
|---|---|---|---|---|
| **Metallurgists** | | | | |
| N.A. | 14 | 18 | 23 | 15 |
| Satisfied | 193 | 191 | 171 | 170 |
| Not Wholly | 19 | 15 | 27 | 26 |
| Dissatisfied | 20 | 22 | 25 | 35 |
| **Other Groups** | | | | |
| N.A. | 9 | 14 | 17 | 12 |
| Satisfied | 188 | 157 | 143 | 144 |
| Not Wholly | 24 | 47 | 54 | 42 |
| Dissatisfied | 25 | 28 | 32 | 48 |

knowledge in the metallurgist's work, it would seem from the replies given that this is not an area of great dissatisfaction. If one classifies the responses into the three categories of satisfied, not wholly satisfied, and dissatisfied, one finds that more than 79 per cent are satisfied when comparing themselves with other groups, and a few more, 83 per cent, when doing so with other metallurgists. On the whole there are no wide differences between the in-group and out-group comparisons, except in the case of Fellows, who are somewhat less satisfied with the latter. The reason for this is an increase in the number who are not wholly satisfied. There are in fact more Fellows who are dissatisfied with the comparison with their metallurgical colleagues. Associates are overall a little less satisfied than Fellows on this, but much more with the in-group than the out-group comparison, whilst Licentiates are clearly the least satisfied of all. This last fact may appear somewhat strange, considering that this group contains those who are employed more than the others on technical work, where their professional knowledge is most likely to be used. The dissatisfaction, which in any case affects only a third, probably arises because they are employed on fairly routine work which they feel could be done by someone with less training than themselves. There are many in the other grades who are quite content even though their professional knowledge is being used very little, but there is, of course, no reason why this should not be so.

Satisfaction with status varies a good deal more between the two reference groups. A high proportion (84 per cent) say that they are satisfied when comparing themselves with their colleagues, but this falls to only 68 per cent when the comparison is with outsiders, even though this remains a fairly substantial majority. Associates are again a little less satisfied than Fellows, especially with the out-group comparison, and the Licentiates are the least satisfied of all. With the latter the difference between the two reference groups is most marked. Although 78 per cent are satisfied when compared to other metallurgists, only 60 per cent are when the comparison is with outside groups. These facts suggest that the dissatisfaction with status is concerned with the position of the whole group, rather than with that of the individual within the group.

When one considers separately those who are engaged in different types of work, the important fact emerges that there is a greater degree of dissatisfaction amongst those in non-management positions than amongst those in management. This holds to some extent for both the in-group and out-group comparisons, but the difference between the proportions who are satisfied is wider for the latter than for the former. Those in management express much the same degree of satisfaction with both, whereas the non-managerial respondents are a good deal less satisfied when they compare themselves to outsiders. Since the former group have had a 'successful' career, and are now identified with the occupational group of administrators rather than of metallurgists, this is not surprising. However, the greater dissatisfaction of the non-management group provides evidence of less favourable employment experience, the situation in which status attitudes should be less strongly held.

The position is clearer if the respondents are split according to the technical content of their work. Those doing the more technical work should be most likely to be cut off from authority and to feel themselves cut off, that is, most likely to develop a class ideology. There is undoubtedly a lower level of satisfaction amongst this group (Table 4), but this time the division is

TABLE 4

*Satisfaction with Status by Technical Content*

|  | Technical | Administrative |
|---|---|---|
| Compared with: | | |
| Metallurgists[1] | | |
| Satisfied | 128 | 36 |
| Dissatisfied: Number | 18 | 1 |
| Per cent | 12·3 | 2·7 |
| Other Groups[2] | | |
| Satisfied | 102 | 32 |
| Dissatisfied: Number | 22 | 3 |
| Per cent | 17·5 | 8·6 |

much more pronounced with the in-group comparison, which would suggest that those doing technical work are more likely to be doubly dissatisfied.

The proportion of satisfied respondents is seen to be somewhat less when opportunities for promotion are considered, though they still form a majority. Taking all members together, 75 per cent are satisfied when compared to other metallurgists, but only 62 per cent when compared with the outside reference group. Dissatisfaction with the position of the group seems to be greater than dissatisfaction with the position of the individual within the group, but there is now more of the latter than there was in the case of status. This is to be expected, since promotion

[1] $\chi^2 = 4·067$: $0·05 > p > 0·02$.
[2] $\chi^2 = 2·494$: $0·20 > p > 0·10$.

is something which depends much more on personal qualities than on membership of a particular group. There are again differences between the grades, with Licentiates having a greater degree of dissatisfaction than the others. There is also a narrower difference between the proportions satisfied with the in- and out-group comparisons, 60 and 67 per cent respectively, than is the case with Fellows, where the proportions are 67 and 90 per cent. Associates occupy an intermediate position. It would thus seem to be the younger, lesser-qualified members who are more likely to be dissatisfied both as individuals and as metallurgists, whilst the older, more qualified members, many of whom will already have had fairly successful careers, are likely to be much more dissatisfied as members of the group than they are as individuals.

It is with salaries that the lowest degrees of satisfaction are found. This is the area in which the lowest proportion are satisfied when colleagues are taken as the reference group, though even here it is still 73 per cent, a sizeable majority. The proportion satisfied with the comparison with outsiders is also one of the lowest at 62 per cent. In view of these figures for members as a whole, it is rather surprising that Licentiates, who elsewhere have been consistently less satisfied than the other grades, give results on the in-group comparison which are very much closer to them. In fact they are rather more satisfied with salaries than Associates. This grade and the Fellows show unusual signs of dissatisfaction, and it would be interesting here to know with whom the dissatisfied ones are comparing themselves. If it is with people of the same age and grade it is difficult to see why there should be more dissatisfaction here than in the other areas. If, however, they are comparing themselves with members of the Institution as a whole, it may be that although they are perhaps better off in absolute terms, they feel that there has been a lowering of differentials between themselves and the younger members. This lowering of differentials would also explain the higher degree of satisfaction amongst Licentiates.

It would be wrong, nevertheless, to imagine a straightforward correlation between age and satisfaction with salary when compared with other metallurgists. It is not, in fact, the very youngest but the middle age-groups which are the most satisfied, so that the lowering of differentials has probably taken place between the top and the middle rather than between the bottom and the rest.

The comparison of salaries with outside groups shows, as the previous results would lead one to expect, a more marked dissatisfaction. Despite the fact that a large proportion of the Licentiates seem satisfied with the comparison with their colleagues, a minority of them, 48 per cent, are satisfied with the position when compared with outsiders. The very wide difference between the two proportions suggests that in this case there is much more group than individual dissatisfaction. If the argument about differentials is correct, it would seem that while Licentiates are satisfied that these have lowered within the professional group of metallurgists themselves, they are far from satisfied with the differentials existing outside—either that those whom they consider equally qualified are doing better than metallurgists, or that other less qualified groups are approaching their own standards too closely.

As with status, there is with salary less satisfaction amongst technical than administrative employees (Table 5). Although

## TABLE 5

### Satisfaction with Salary by Technical Content

| Compared with: | Technical | Administrative |
|---|---|---|
| Metallurgists[1] | | |
| Satisfied | 110 | 35 |
| Dissatisfied: Number | 28 | 2 |
| Per cent | 22·9 | 5·4 |
| Other Groups[2] | | |
| Satisfied | 92 | 30 |
| Dissatisfied: Number | 35 | 7 |
| Per cent | 27·6 | 18·9 |

this is true for both the in-group and out-group comparisons, it is much more positive for the former than the latter, which is hardly significant. The reason for the difference is that those in administration show a much higher degree of dissatisfaction when comparing themselves to outsiders, which suggests that theirs is more a dissatisfaction with the situation of the whole group than with their own individual position.

[1] $\chi^2 = 5\cdot659$: $p < 0\cdot025$.
[2] $\chi^2 = 1\cdot622$: $0\cdot30 > p > 0\cdot20$.

The overall impression gained from the consideration of the metallurgists' views on these four aspects of their employment is that satisfaction is in general quite high. Consistently, there has been found a lower degree of satisfaction when the comparison is with outside groups than when it is with colleagues. The former is in many ways more important, since an individual is more likely to concern himself with his place in the wider socio-economic structure than with his position within the occupational group. The difference is less marked for those doing technical work than for those in administration. For the former, dissatisfaction, where it exists, is most likely to be two-fold. Those in administration, when they are dissatisfied because of their inferior position to outsiders, are usually able to get consolation from comparing themselves with their colleagues. Many of them, in fact, are probably not thinking of their own position at all as much as of that of metallurgists in general. There is, therefore, strong evidence that those in technical work are the least satisfied.

In each of the four areas considered there is a relationship between satisfaction and the grade of membership, such that Licentiates are consistently less satisfied and Fellows more, with Associates spread between them. The highest proportion of Licentiates who are satisfied is still less than the lowest proportion of Fellows. However, there is a basically similar pattern in the order of satisfaction with these four areas. With the out-group comparison the main difference is that whereas Fellows and Associates are least satisfied with opportunities for promotion and then with salaries, Licentiates reverse this order. When the in-group comparison is considered the differences are greater. Thus Fellows are least satisfied with salary, followed by status, whereas status and salary are the areas in which Licentiates are most satisfied. Like the Fellows, Associates are most dissatisfied with salaries, but next for them comes opportunities for promotion, which is also the area of least satisfaction for Licentiates. Both Fellows and Associates are most satisfied with the use made of their professional knowledge, whereas for Licentiates this is an area of least satisfaction.

The extent to which members are satisfied with these four aspects of their employment has been considered, now it is necessary to see whether they think that the Institution should concern itself with them. As regards the first aspect, the use made of professional knowledge, taking all members together, 52 per cent think that the Institution should do more about this, and 5 per cent that it should do less or nothing at all. If one separates the grades there emerge clear differences between them, with the lower grades wanting more action—44 per cent of Fellows, 53 per cent of Associates and 66 per cent of Licentiates.

There is a relationship between a desire for more action and dissatisfaction with this aspect, though the number who want more done, being so large, must obviously include many of those who are satisfied. In fact, considering first of all the in-group comparison, 49 per cent of these want more done, compared with 65 per cent of those who are not wholly satisfied and 83 per cent of those who are dissatisfied. For the out-group comparison the correlation is even higher, the respective proportions being 49 per cent, 73 per cent and 91 per cent. This fact, that dissatisfaction with the out-group comparison is more strongly related to wanting the Institution to do more in this matter, tends to support the argument that it is seen more as a body to deal with the general problems of metallurgists as a whole than with those of individuals.

In the case of status a slightly higher proportion of all respondents (54 per cent) think that the Institution should concern itself more, and only 4 per cent that it should concern itself less. These few are typified by the respondent who wrote that 'status accrues to individuals worthy of it. Any Institution cheapens itself by concerning itself with so sterile an entity as status.'

There are not such marked differences between grades in this matter, and this time it is the Associates who want more done, 64 per cent of them, compared with 55 per cent of Licentiates and 48 per cent of Fellows. It was this area, it will be remembered, in which Licentiates are most satisfied. The correlation between the degrees of satisfaction and wanting more done is not as marked either. The highest proportion wanting more activity are amongst those who are not wholly satisfied rather than those who are dissatisfied, in both the in-group and out-group comparisons, though the lowest proportions are still found amongst those who express themselves as satisfied.

Promotion is the aspect of their work in which the smallest

number of members think that the Institution should take more interest. There is, in fact, a sizeable minority who think that it should concern itself less than it now does or even not at all—14 per cent. The respondent quoted above is this time a little more representative in his belief that 'prospects for promotion are governed by the operation of the market. Unless an Institution becomes an employer it cannot influence market forces.' Nevertheless, just under one-half, 42 per cent, of all members do think that it should show more concern. Once again, Associates are the most likely to desire greater interest from the Institution—48 per cent, as compared with 39 per cent of Licentiates and only 26 per cent of Fellows. The usual tendency for the less satisfied to show a higher proportion wanting more done is less marked here, although it is clearer for the out-group than the in-group comparison.

Very slightly less than one-half of the members (47 per cent) want the Institution to concern itself more with salaries, and only 5 per cent think that it should do less—for example the respondent who stated that 'if, and this I most strongly doubt, the officers of the Institution wish to be mistaken for gentlemen they would be well advised to avoid an undue concern for the contents of other people's pay packets'. Licentiates and Associates have approximately the same proportions wanting more activity, 56 and 53 per cent respectively, but it is much lower with Fellows, 37 per cent. In this area there is a high correlation between dissatisfaction and the desire that more be done, whether one considers the in-group or the out-group comparison.

There is, as has already been seen, a relationship between the type of work done and dissatisfaction with both status and salary, and now a relationship has been shown to exist between these dissatisfactions and wanting the Institution to do more. It is, therefore, rather surprising that the relationship between type of work and wanting more done, although it exists, is not a very marked one. Of those doing technical work 54 per cent want more done about salary, 60 per cent more done about status, whereas for those in administration the respective figures are 40 per cent and 47 per cent. Although not very significant, the relationships are nevertheless positive, and it is interesting that the division between the two groups is more clear-cut in the case of salary than it is with status.

Despite the degree of satisfaction with their work which members have shown, therefore, there is still a large proportion who would like the Institution to concern itself more than it now does with the four aspects of their employment. Except in the case of opportunities for promotion there is, taking all members together, a small majority wanting more activity on each of these matters. Only amongst Fellows are those who want more done in a minority. The great majority of the remainder of the respondents feel that the Institution should go on as it now does, with only a very few thinking that it should do nothing at all.

The area in which the largest proportion believe that more should be done is status, with the use made of professional knowledge some way below and salary a little below this. Taking each grade separately, only Licentiates differ from this pattern. Their greatest demand is for more to be done about the use made of their knowledge and skill, something with which they are quite strongly dissatisfied when comparing themselves to their colleagues, so that this is a matter which they probably believe can best be dealt with internally by the Institution. After this they want more done about salaries, with status just a little way behind.

There is no obvious correlation between dissatisfaction with any particular aspect and wanting more done about it. The main consideration seems to be whether the matter is a suitable one for the Institution to deal with. For the whole group it is obvious that they consider status rather than salaries to be the main area with which the Institution should and could concern itself more. This emphasis on status is, in terms of the present thesis, significant. In part it reflects a desire for more status alone, for example the respondent who thought that the Institution should do more about salaries 'in so far as this reflects on status–but not purely for financial return'. Others want the Institution to pursue both higher status and higher salaries, seeing that the two are connected, as does the respondent who believes that financial reward 'is, or should be, tied up with status and therefore [the Institution should do] more than it does now'. There are those who would rather it concerned itself more only with status, even though their main interest seems to be in higher salaries: 'As it does now, since if the status of the profession were increased, higher financial rewards would probably follow.'

PROFESSIONAL PEOPLE-1

Some respondents are doubtful about the relationship between status and salary as far as the activities of the Institution are concerned. They see the danger of a concern with salary leading to trade unionism. There is, for example, the respondent who wants more done about salaries, but only in the sense of 'promotion of the idea that metallurgists are a deserving class and should have higher rewards'. 'I believe in individual enterprise', he says, and 'if I can get a higher salary than a co-worker by legitimate means then I want freedom to attempt this. I do not want a trade union.' A similar idea comes from the one who says that: 'I do not think that the Institution should become too deeply involved, and would not welcome any tendency to try to obtain Trade Union powers in this respect', even though he too would like the Institution to concern itself more with salaries. There is clearly a less wholehearted desire for more to be done about salaries than there is for status.

However, since so many of the members think that the Institution should concern itself more with these four aspects of their work, it is interesting to see how they suggest that it should go about it. They were not asked what they thought should be done about each one separately, but about the four in general. The responses naturally tend to be rather similar to those given in answer to the question on what further activities they would like to see undertaken by the Institution, except that in this case they were prompted to answer within the context of their satisfaction or dissatisfaction with the four aspects of their work.

Of the total membership, 54 per cent gave a definite answer to this question, ranging from 42 per cent of Fellows to 55 per cent of Associates and 59 per cent of Licentiates. The most common method suggested, by 22 per cent (of those who gave an answer), is publicity. It is given more often by Licentiates than by Associates, and more by these than by Fellows. The publicity is to be aimed at management, the government or the general public, and seems to be seen largely as a means of raising status.

'By greater publicity of its achievements to higher management who are not metallurgists.'
'It should adopt a more pugnacious attitude, seeking every opportunity to make use of publicity.'

'Should aim to increase public knowledge of the metallurgical profession, i.e. articles in the press, reviews of problems and current work on radio and T.V.'

An only slightly less popular response is that the Institution should do more in the educational field, in various ways, which would enable the individual members to be more successful in competition, especially with outsiders. This suggestion is given less by Associates than by the other grades. Some stress the need to maintain or raise the examination standards, others would like a wider syllabus.

'By raising the standards required to obtain either L.I.M., A.I.M. or F.I.M. and also by widening the scope of knowledge required so that metallurgists are not so specialized as at present.'

'The Institution's examinations should place greater emphasis on the scientific fundamentals, e.g. physics, chemistry and maths. Given a firm, broad foundation, the subsequent metallurgical experience found in industry will do much to enable a man to avoid a narrow specialization. Promotion will follow. If my earlier remarks are true the individual will benefit without the necessity for the I. of M. to push for "status" as such.'

These responses shade over into the next most common one, given by 10 per cent and particularly favoured by Fellows, that the Institution should encourage more 'general education' in management, even in the arts and humanities, which they think would be much more useful for a successful career, that is one of promotion to management, than more technical training. This suggestion, obviously, is particularly aimed at improving prospects for promotion.

'It should concern itself more with management by including this as a subject in its examination syllabus and to include it in refresher courses etc. Management ability should then automatically lead to improved status, prospects for promotion and financial rewards.'

Other responses are much more concerned with what the Institution can do as a representative body rather than as a provider of services to its members. These go as far as advocating that it should lay down a scale of minimum salaries for metallurgists (9·5 per cent), a response which is given most often by Licentiates and much less by Fellows. It can represent some rather different attitudes, as the following examples show.

'The salary survey should be more widely circulated and the Institution should indicate what they consider the average member of each grade should be earning.'

'The Institution could reasonably fix minimum salaries for its various members and could act as an arbitrator between employer and employed. I believe that the Law Society and also the General Medical Council fix minimum fees and remuneration for its members—why not the Institution of Metallurgists? Unless one desires to join trade unions with *political affiliations* there is no collective body of metallurgists to deal with various financial maladjustments. There should be facilities for negotiation at both local and national level on these matters.' ('I deplore the fact, and so do many of my colleagues and acquaintances, that the earning capacity of labourers, semi-skilled workers both male and female, can be considerably higher than the earning capacity of highly qualified, highly experienced metallurgists.')

Very close to this response, but less extreme, is the idea that the Institution should draw conclusions from the salary surveys, instead of merely presenting them as factual statements (4 per cent). Others, more vaguely, think that the Institution should deal with salaries (8 per cent), some of the respondents obviously thinking of other professional groups.

'Suggest development along lines of Guild of Engineers, to be able to negotiate salaries and conditions of employment for members.'

'The Institution should try and copy the methods of the British Medical Association and elevate the status and financial rewards of the profession as the B.M.A. has done for the medical profession.'

Other respondents (9 per cent) suggest that the Institution should consult with government bodies and managements about these matters, on the lines of the following examples.

'They might well educate employers and prospective employers as to the value of metallurgists.'

'I feel management in general should be made more aware of the conditions which obtain in other professions.

'Encourage management to use technically trained people for administration—where circumstances permit.'

This response is specially popular with Associates, but is little mentioned by Licentiates. A milder suggestion, given by a few, is that salary surveys should be conducted more frequently. Taken together these various related responses account for 36 per cent of the total. As has been said, those doing technical work are only slightly more eager that the Institution should concern itself more with these four matters, but it is significant that they form the great majority of those who give these more 'radical' responses. Many members want the Institution to do more about all of these things, but it is those doing technical work who are most likely to suggest the sort of means which show signs of class attitudes.

The main emphasis of these professional people is clearly on status, which is most influential in determining their opinions. Nevertheless, there are tendencies towards class attitudes amongst certain groups, especially those who want the Institution to engage in more activities concerned with the protective function. Since it is this function, and the tendencies towards class attitudes, which are of central importance to our study, it is necessary to pursue the problems further, as we shall do in the following chapter when the Engineers' Guild is considered.

# CHAPTER SIX

# Professional People—2

## THE ENGINEERS' GUILD

A good deal has already been said about the activities and functions of the Engineers' Guild in Chapter 4. It is not itself a qualifying body, but it accepts for membership only corporate members of the recognized engineering Institutions. One of its main declared aims is 'to do for engineers what the B.M.A. does for doctors', and it is in this claim that much of its interest lies. Since the professional protective function is separated from the technical and qualifying functions, the Guild is in the position of having to achieve sufficient results to attract and hold its members, without undertaking the sort of activities which members would think unprofessional. Where the profession is composed of independent practitioners, there is no problem, since the professional group can control admission to the profession and the fees charged. But when, as with engineers, the great majority are employees, there is an obvious possibility that professional protection will merge into trade-union collective bargaining. Indeed, some form of negotiation with an employer seems to be the only possible effective method of furthering their financial interests collectively. As has been seen, most of the other professional bodies concern themselves very little with the protective function. For the Guild, however, this is its main reason for existence, and therefore, if our thesis is correct, it should be shown to be either a largely ineffective body, not fulfilling its avowed function, or to be moving towards more collective bargaining, that is, class activity. If one reverts to the Guild's own chosen example, the B.M.A., it is clear that since the advent of the National Health Service the nature of the employment of the great majority of doctors has changed. As a result of their own pressures during the drawing-up of the Bill they are not, it is true, salaried employees, but independent professionals whose fees are paid by the State. The distinction, however, is more one of principle than practice, and has not prevented the growth of a system of collective bargaining between the B.M.A. and the Treasury, which, though it may differ from other systems, must surely be acknowledged as such.[1]

The Engineers' Guild, however, is still not in the same position as the B.M.A. Engineers are not, like doctors, employed almost exclusively by the State or any other single large employer, but are widely distributed throughout many different industries, local and central government and Education, as was seen in the third chapter. They are also more obviously salaried employees than are doctors, and these two facts, the wide diversity of employment and the lack of the formal independence of the doctors, have prevented the growth of any similar system of bargaining. Earlier in its history, at the beginning of the 1950's, the Guild seemed to be moving in this direction wherever possible but it came up against the double difficulty of its own insufficient representation and the existence of other stronger more definitely trade-union bodies. Recently the official opinion of the Guild has swung clearly away from collective bargaining towards a more professional attitude. Later parts of this chapter will show how far this view is shared by the members, and where it is, what they see as the necessary sorts of activity involved in the professional protective function.

The total membership of the Guild may be taken as an expression of the recognition of its value by the engineering profession as a whole. Accepting the Guild's own definition of the profession at the time this study was made their potential membership is in the region of 100,000, whilst their actual membership is around 5,000—only 5 per cent. Of course there is truth in the Guild's arguments that they have so low a proportion of the potential membership because their power is limited, and that this is because of their low numbers. They are caught in a vicious circle, but so at the beginning are most such bodies, and many of these have managed to break out of it.

[1] For a thorough study of this, see H. Eckstein, *Pressure Group Politics*, Allen and Unwin, 1960.

The fact that the Guild has existed for over 15 years, excluding the period of the last war, without doing so is surely evidence that most professional engineers are satisfied with their lot, or, if they are not, that they do not see the Guild as the sort of body which would be able to do anything about it. Naturally, this does not exclude the possibility that, with a change in circumstances, the Guild could greatly increase its membership and power at any time in the future, but such a change might also necessitate a change in the types of activities carried out. As it is, it is not clear what the Guild would do even if it had a very high membership. It would then, after all, be in a position very much like that of the Institution of Metallurgists, which still does not concern itself greatly with the protective function.

## EDUCATIONAL AND WORK BACKGROUND

Nevertheless, some engineers have joined the Guild, and because of the importance of this body in illustrating the pressures on salaried professionals already discussed, it is valuable to know something about them. Unfortunately, it is difficult when looking at the background of members of the Guild to say how far this differs from that of the engineering profession as a whole, because there is only a little information available on the characteristics of engineers in general. There is, however, one recent, unpublished study of the engineering profession by McFarlane which is of value.[1]

The information for this chapter was gained from interviewing all (except two refusals) 44 members of the Guild in the Merseyside area. Further details of the methods used are to be found in the Appendix.

One fact emerges obviously at the very outset, that the proportions of the three types of engineer in the Guild (there were no chemical engineers in our survey—they are anyway only a very small group) differ from the total proportions. Electrical

[1] B. A. McFarlane, ' *The Chartered Engineer*: a study of the recruitment, qualification, conditions of employment, and professional associations of chartered Civil, Electrical and Mechanical Engineers in Great Britain', unpublished Ph.D. thesis, London, 1961. Unless otherwise stated, this work, especially chapters 4 and 5, is the source of comparative material for the whole engineering profession used in this chapter.

and mechanical engineers, especially the former, are under-represented, while civil engineers are very much over-represented. This fact alone says a good deal about the Guild, for civil engineers are in several ways different from the others. They are the oldest of the branches of engineering, the one in which there is the largest proportion of independent practitioners, and probably the most professionally-minded. There is a general impression, which unfortunately cannot be fully documented, that civil engineers are not only senior but superior to the others, and enjoy a higher status. Certainly they are recruited from somewhat higher social strata, and tend much more to take the full-time, mostly university, route to qualification. On the other hand, despite this cachet, they are on average the worst paid, mainly because a high proportion of them work for local authorities. They are thus faced with two contradictory pressures, one towards heightened professional feeling and the other towards collective bargaining, which is strong amongst local government employees. This combination of pressures, however, could easily lead an individual to join the Guild, which would seem to him to offer some sort of resolution of them, precisely because it is itself in the same ambivalent position.

This fact, that there is an unduly high proportion of civil engineers, also affects several other aspects of the background of members. Thus, for example, 9 of the 13 respondents employed by public bodies are civil engineers. The majority of each of the other types are in private industry, with the electrical engineers mostly in electrical engineering, and the mechanical engineers in the chemicals, glass, and food industries. One would expect there to be some mechanical engineers in the Guild employed in the plant and machinery industry, but their absence may be due to the pattern of employment in the Merseyside area, where there are not many examples of this type of industry.

A large proportion of civil engineers are employed on construction and maintenance work, the type of work carried out by 42 per cent of all those interviewed. There are also 18 per cent each in management and in research and development, mostly mechanical engineers. A few more are in sales, nearly all electrical engineers, and in education and other types of work. Considering the technical content of their work, half the members are doing jobs which are wholly or mainly technical, but whereas there are equal numbers of civil engineers in technical and administrative work, with the other two types there are nearly twice as many of each in the former.

The educational experience of the members suggests a fairly high social background. Nearly a half of the total group attended university, and exactly one-half have degrees. Nearly two-thirds went to grammar school, and a quarter to public school. This is a very high proportion, partly explained by the over-representation of civil engineers, who comprise almost one-half of the public-school group. This fact provides further evidence towards the view mentioned above that civil engineers enjoy a higher status within the whole engineering profession. Whether the ex-public-school boys are over-represented in the Guild is difficult to judge, probably they are a little. It must be borne in mind, however, that, according to McFarlane in the study mentioned earlier, a half of all chartered engineers had fathers in the Hall-Jones categories 1 and 2.

For the whole group, graduates seem to be represented in the expected proportion, but this in fact masks different patterns for the three types of engineer. Comparing the Guild members with all engineers, it seems that graduate civil engineers are slightly under-represented (56 per cent as against 68 per cent), electrical engineers very much under-represented (17 per cent to 32 per cent) and mechanical engineers very much over-represented (55 per cent to 25 per cent). In other words, the Guild seems to attract different sections, in terms of qualifications, of the three types of engineers. This suggests that it is attracting them for different reasons, and we shall have occasion to return to this point later.

It is difficult, because of the small numbers involved, to establish any correlation for the Guild members between education or qualification and the type of work performed, or a successful career. However, in this latter respect, some idea of the position of the whole profession can be gained from McFarlane, who concludes that more of those from elementary school were likely to be 'least successful' (in terms of salary), and many more of those from public schools, especially, and also from universities, to be 'very successful'.

## ATTITUDES TOWARDS THE GUILD

Firstly, what are the reasons given by the members for joining the Guild? The most common response (Table 1) is

### TABLE 1

*Reasons for Joining the Guild*

| | |
|---|---|
| Improve Status | 12 |
| Deal with Salaries, etc. | 7 |
| 'Good Idea' | 7 |
| Bargaining Body | 5 |
| Persuaded | 5 |
| Representation | 4 |
| Social | 2 |
| Other | 3 |

that they did so in order to help improve the status of engineers, or at least to support a body which they thought might do this.

'I thought that engineers needed an association, not a trade union to boost their status. Like the B.M.A.'

'In the early days engineers were looked up to. Between the wars this declined. I thought the Guild would improve the situation.'

'Dissatisfaction with the status of professional engineers. I expected no immediate gain, but knew that this depended on increased membership.'

This is quite as much a desire for an improvement in the position of the whole profession as for the individual himself. In fact it is probably more so, with most members anticipating only a possible indirect benefit to themselves.

The next most popular response is much more concerned with individual benefit, the member saying he joined because he thought of the Guild as a body which could deal with salaries and conditions of employment.

'I was in the Colonial Service at the time and conditions of service were not satisfactory, especially compared to those in administration.'

'Engineers were badly paid, and the Guild was the only body concerned with this.'

A slightly smaller group saw it as a body which would not merely deal with but actually bargain over these matters.

> 'Collective bargaining has its advantages. Engineers are poorly paid and their status is not recognized.'

Some of these were already members of another trade union which they considered inappropriate for them.

> 'I was virtually forced to be a member of the E.P.E.A. (though I was averse to trade unions), which covers all grades, and I thought that the Guild would be a more suitable body for negotiating for qualified engineers. As yet, though, it does not.'

Other responses are much more general and vague than these. For example, the fairly substantial proportion who thought the Guild to be 'a good idea'.

> 'I felt that the Guild at least deserved a trial, though I wasn't entirely sold on the idea since I don't want a union. I'm still a member because it has not yet proved to be not useful.'

A few are a little disillusioned.

> 'It put over such a wonderful story, that it would be like the B.M.A.'

Another rather vague group are those who joined because they were persuaded to by another member. Others became members for the general reason of obtaining 'representation', without any specific explanation of what they thought this entailed, and a few of the rest for the social activities, the chance to meet other engineers informally which the Guild provides.

Obviously many Guild members are concerned with status, and a status ideology has a good deal of influence on their attitudes. Nevertheless, there are almost as many who lean further towards class ideas, represented by those who joined because they wanted the Guild to deal with salaries, or because they wanted it to be a bargaining body. These class responses are not randomly distributed. There is, for example, a difference between the younger and older groups in their reason for joining. Of those born before 1920, 36 per cent give the class type of response, compared with only 16 per cent of those born after this date.

There are differences, also, between the types of engineers. Proportionately more civil engineers joined the Guild as a body to deal with salaries and conditions, and electrical engineers lean more towards the idea of the Guild as a bargaining body. Mechanical engineers, on the other hand, give the more 'professional' responses of a desire to improve the status of engineers and the need for representation. To some extent the differences reflect the industries in which the members are employed. The class responses, those mentioning bargaining and dealing with salaries and conditions, are given mostly by those employed in water supply and transport, in which civil engineers predominate, and electricity supply and electrical engineering, naturally comprising mostly electrical engineers. Except for the last of these they are all run by public bodies, in which there is already an extensive system of collective bargaining. An example has already been given to show how some members see the Guild as a body which could be at once extensive, by representing all engineers, and exclusive, by giving them special representation as engineers, rather than merely, as at present, leaving them to be negotiated for as just one section of a large trade union dominated by the lower grades. It may also be that they see the Guild as a more respectable sort of body, to deal with salaries, not to bargain over them. It is interesting that a high proportion in electrical engineering should give the bargaining response. Electrical engineers, it may be remembered, are the group with the least full-time education, probably therefore with more members from a lower socio-economic background, to whom this might seem a less 'improper' response. In fact, 4 of the 5 who joined the Guild as a bargaining body had had only a part-time higher education.

The members of the Guild do not seem to make a great deal of use of the services that it provides. Well over one-half say that they have used none, though a few of these think that they would be useful if they ever needed them. Of those that have made some use of the services provided, most used the information and inquiry services, some found the salary surveys of value, and some liked the social activities. Only two had used the Appointments Bureau, and these had not found it of much help.

Status is clearly the main single concern of the members when they consider the Guild's function for the professional, as can be seen from Table 2. Over 40 per cent of the responses say

### TABLE 2
*Views on Guild's Function**

| | |
|---|---|
| Raise Status | 18 |
| Deal with Salaries, etc. | 11 |
| Look after Interests | 6 |
| Get Recognition | 6 |
| Publicize Engineers | 3 |
| Other | 4 |

*Some multiple responses

that the Guild's major function is to raise the status of the engineering profession. Nearly one-quarter, however, thought that it should concern itself directly with salaries and conditions, rather than with status.

> 'To persuade industry to pay the engineer his worth.'
> 'To give bargaining if it is required. It could be like a trade union or the B.M.A.'

Other responses were closely allied to one or the other of these. One was that it should look after the interests of engineers, which could be taken as meaning their interests in a general way, or their particular social or financial interests. The suggestions that the Guild should obtain public recognition of engineers, and that it should publicize their activities and achievements, are similarly perhaps an indirect way of implying that engineers are not sufficiently rewarded either in terms of social esteem or financially.

When it comes to suggesting ways in which the Guild could be improved, and new activities that it could undertake, the members have little to say. A number can suggest nothing at all, whilst the majority of those who do give only the obvious reply, though in this case it is also a reasonable one, that it should try to get more members. Of the others there are a few who would like it to undertake definite negotiating and representation activities, or who less specifically ask for it to be more forthright.

Those interviewed, whatever their own reason for joining, are almost unanimous in believing that all engineers should become members of the Guild. All but the few who think that they should join because it would be in their own interest, see more members as leading to more strength for the Guild. They recognize, however, that many other engineers do not join because they see no benefit to themselves. This is the most frequent reason given for why others do not join (32 per cent), with the next most popular that they are too apathetic (16 per cent). This is really closely allied to the first response, since presumably if the benefits were obvious enough they would be stirred out of their apathy. Allied to it also is the response that they have no need of it, that they do quite well for themselves without. A few are concerned more with the Guild as a bargaining body; that other engineers do not join either because it does not negotiate or because they already have other trade unions–answers which come mainly from those employed in public bodies. These responses, however, are outnumbered by the contradictory ones which suggest that many engineers do not join the Guild because they see it as a trade union and are against trade unions on principle.

## WORK AND THE GUILD

It would seem from Table 3 that those engineers who join

### TABLE 3

*Satisfaction with Use Made of Skill, Status, Prospects for Promotion and Salary*

|  | Skill | Status | Promotion | Salary |
|---|---|---|---|---|
| Satisfied | 40 | 34 | 30 | 31 |
| Not Wholly | — | 5 | 3 | 6 |
| Dissatisfied | 4 | 5 | 11 | 7 |

the Guild do not do so because they are particularly dissatisfied with any of the four aspects of their employment which have already been considered in the previous chapter. The area of greatest dissatisfaction is with prospects for promotion, but even here nearly three-quarters say that they are satisfied. However, this means that there are a quarter dissatisfied and a few more who are not wholly satisfied. Financial reward is the area of next to lowest satisfaction. Here there is only one more individual who is satisfied, but fewer who are completely dissatisfied. Slightly more again are satisfied with status, and it is rather surprising that this should be so in view of the importance they attach to the Guild's function of improving status. The fact that they are personally less dissatisfied with this than with prospects for promotion and salaries suggests that it is these reflections of status with which they are really most concerned. The great majority are satisfied with the use made of their professional knowledge and skill.

Certain differences between sub-groups within the Guild have already been described in analysing the reasons why members joined the Guild. It was seen then that some groups showed a greater tendency to give responses of a class type, and it is interesting to see that these same groups are the least satisfied members. In fact, although they are described as groups, they are basically the same group whose education, background and employment are closely related and all tending to lead to greater dissatisfaction.

Dealing first with education, the most significant division is between those with full and those with part-time higher education. If the proportions of those dissatisfied in each group (counting 'not wholly satisfied' as one-half dissatisfied) are compared, then the only area in which the two groups are similar is in prospects for promotion–29 per cent of the part-time group and 28 per cent of the full-time. They differ most widely in their dissatisfaction with the use made of their skill (18 per cent and 4 per cent), but it is notable that they also differ more widely over salary (38 and 13 per cent) than over status (23·5 and 13 per cent). The part-time group, those on the whole with the lower socio-economic background, are therefore the ones most likely to be dissatisfied with their actual salary, less likely to be dissatisfied with their status.

When the three types of engineer are compared, the most significant result is the higher proportion of electrical engineers who are dissatisfied with their salary–48 per cent, compared with only 15 per cent of mechanical and 12·5 per cent of civil engineers.

Finally, a comparison of those doing technical and those doing administrative work again shows up differences. Only a small proportion of the former are dissatisfied with the use made of their skill, but none of the latter are. Clearly those who have moved into administrative posts are quite happy about having little use made of their technical skill. However, it is the question of salaries which is most interesting. The difference between the two groups over satisfaction with status (18 per cent compared to 13 per cent) again is not as significant as the differences over salary, where those in technical work are over twice as much dissatisfied—27 per cent compared with 13 per cent.

Nevertheless, although status is not the area in which members showed the greatest dissatisfaction, it is the one in which they would most like to see the Guild do more. Nearly three-quarters think that it should concern itself more with status, and very nearly as many think that it should concern itself more with salaries. This supports the arguments already made that the Guild is seen by most as a body to deal with status, that is, it is seen in terms of a status ideology, but at the same time there is an almost equal tendency to want it to deal with salaries, something which is more likely to lead to activities of a class type. Far fewer members believe that the Guild should do more about prospects for promotion or the use made of professional skill, presumably because these are taken to be outside the scope of a representative body of this sort, even though the first of these areas was the one of greatest dissatisfaction.

Since so many are of the opinion that the Guild should concern itself more about one or other of these matters, it is useful to know that suggestions are made as to how it might do so. The most frequent (9 responses) is that it should make representations to managements, a response which indicates at least some move away from a pure status ideology. Some idea of what is meant by this response can be gained from the following examples.

> 'By direct contact with larger industrial organizations, and giving information on salaries in the profession and outside it to firms and the engineers employed in them.'
>
> 'By direct intervention with management if a problem arises.'

Almost as popular (8) was the desire for more publicity, which is particularly related to the concern over status and the opinion in which engineers are held by the general public. Many feel that the Guild should help to educate the public so that they would have a much clearer idea of what engineers do, and especially to distinguish the qualified man from the great mass of skilled and semi-skilled craftsmen popularly known as 'engineers'.

> 'By pointing out the meaning of engineering to newspapers, and to educate the public by publicity.'
> 'By advertising, to stress engineers' achievements and to show the difference from other "engineers".'

A few go even further, to suggest that the Guild should press for some method of registering qualified engineers and getting for them a legally protected title, or at least a more definite one. This is designed not only as a means of overcoming the public confusion over the real meaning of the term engineer, but also as a means of enhancing the profession's status, making it more like that of doctors and architects by excluding those who are not qualified from being employed as engineers.

> 'By statutory registration of engineers.'
> 'The general public doesn't know what an engineer is. There should be a title for chartered engineers.'

The most 'radical' response, given by a few, is an outright statement that the Guild should undertake collective bargaining.

> 'Start a salary policy, and then later begin negotiation. It should concern itself less with pure ideals.'
> 'Get representation on negotiating bodies, though this is difficult to do.'

Others suggest action through conducting salary surveys, using the Appointments Bureau, providing advisory services ('Not by poking its nose in, but by gaining a knowledge of what is going on and giving advice to individuals'), and getting more members.

Although only a few respondents think that the Guild should undertake negotiating activities, this does not seem to mean that most of them are against collective bargaining as a means of dealing with the problems of engineers. Exactly one-half (22 individuals) believe that it is not suitable, a few are doubtful, and the rest think that it is suitable.

The reasons given for their opinions make the matter a little more complex, however. Of those who consider it unsuitable, almost a third do so because they think that for them it does not or would not work.

'Salaries depend on supply and demand, and engineers are now very short. There is no need for negotiation, and anyway it would be difficult because there could be no basic rate or grading system.'

'It can lay down a general scale, but this would be very wide, because jobs are very different. It wouldn't work.'

Less than a quarter (5) object definitely on grounds of principle, that it is not right for professional men, though some of those who give no reason for objecting may feel the same.

'The greater need and better way is to obtain public recognition. Engineers are individualists and won't let an association decide their career.'

'Professional men should look after themselves.'

'It is disgraceful for professionals to strike, for example, teachers. I have doubts about the use of the Guild, but not serious enough to make me think of resigning. Probably it is of some use. The nearest equivalent is the B.M.A.'

Others, who believe that collective bargaining would tend to lower their status and perhaps also their salary, cannot easily be categorized as giving either a practical or a principled objection.

'It protects the bad at the expense of the good.'

'It reduces everyone to one level.'

'I have no desire to be one of a herd.'

'Trade unions are bad for their members, because they lower their status.'

Just as opposition to collective bargaining varies in its nature and intensity, so, on the other hand, does support for it. Ten of the 18 respondents who accept collective bargaining, for example, have reservations, either as to its scope or its nature.

'Not for the whole profession, but the Guild could apply a minimum standard for a given qualification to industry.'

'Yes, though not as done by trade unions. More like N.A.L.G.O., and not forced on all the members.'

'Yes, of a mild sort. I should hate to get to a level of warfare. Sweet reason should prevail.'

A few think it suitable for public bodies, but not in private industry.

> 'It is the only way in the A.E.A. since the Treasury pays their salaries, and any action must be joint.'

Six of this favourable group, however, feel that, for the majority at least, it is the only way.

> 'Yes, because they are employees, and it is the only practicable way. Even the B.M.A. does it.'

> 'It is the only way. Individuals are incapable of finding their own place. It does depend on the size of the industry. It's difficult for an individual to negotiate when he is put in a category by an employer.'

Between these two fairly definite groups are the doubtful ones, those who cannot decide on the suitability of collective bargaining. The following are two examples of such respondents.

> 'My instinct is to say no, but I wonder whether anything else is possible, though I have always been fortunate in my employers. In local government, for example, it can bring order out of chaos.'

> 'Not entirely. It can deal with certain aspects only. The Guild should act as arbitrator in the last resort in a dispute between an employer and an engineer, giving advice to both.'

Educational experience has an influence on the attitude towards collective bargaining. From their responses to other questions it is perhaps not surprising to find that the part-time technical college group are much more in favour than those who had full-time higher education. Sixty per cent of the former think collective bargaining suitable, compared with only 36 per cent of the latter.

Rather surprisingly, it is the civil engineers who are more in favour of bargaining than either of the other types, but this is largely explained by the fact that many of them are employed in public bodies, where the general attitude to collective bargaining is much more favourable. This fact also provides an explanation of why the relationship between doing technical work and being more in favour of collective bargaining is not greater than it is. There is some relationship, since whereas those in administration are two-to-one against bargaining, those doing technical work are equally divided. It seems likely that most of the administrative workers with a favourable attitude are in fact employed in public bodies.

There is, however, an interesting relationship between the attitude towards collective bargaining and the degree of satisfaction with the four aspects of employment already considered. For each of these there exists a clear correlation between dissatisfaction and a more favourable attitude towards bargaining. It is weakest in the case of prospects for promotion, where 50 per cent of the satisfied are in favour, compared with 70 per cent of the dissatisfied. It is more definite for salary (37 and 71 per cent respectively), and most marked with status (33 and 80 per cent).

It might seem that this result could arise from the fact that the least satisfied respondents are the ones who are employed by public bodies and therefore already members of a trade union. Union members, as one would expect, tend much more to consider bargaining as suitable, but there are, in fact, more respondents with a favourable attitude not in a union than there are members. Nor, indeed, is it the union members who are the least satisfied. On the contrary, they are more satisfied in each of the four areas than the non-union members.

The most obvious fact about the Engineers' Guild is really its weakness. Its membership is small, and its power very limited. Whilst its appeal to a majority seems to be as a 'professional body', they themselves holding a status ideology, a substantial minority composed of those with a lower social background and doing technical rather than administrative work, see the Guild much more as a body which should negotiate in some way with management. A status ideology may be uppermost amongst Guild Members, but class attitudes can be seen to be entering very strongly.

# Conclusion

The fact that emerged most clearly from the survey of professional associations was the great emphasis that all of them place on the technical function, the furtherance of the study of their particular specialism. This seemed to be the function with which the associations were most concerned, and indeed the one which the members saw, after qualification, as the most important. In the case of the Institution of Metallurgists, which does not have many study activities, this is the function which most members wanted to see expanded, and the expansion is, in fact, taking place. A similar preoccupation is not found amongst other professional groups, doctors or lawyers for example, and reflects their different origins and situation. Other professional bodies were founded to give representation, those in science and engineering were founded to enable men to get together to share their experience and 'further the study'. This is most obvious in the case of the engineering bodies, which have all followed the pattern set by the Big Three. Even the function of qualification, which the members see as the most important, is only a later addition, still arising in part out of the concern for the advancement of the field of study.

The foundation of each association shows a close relationship with the practical, industrial application of the study. This has been largely true from the beginning with civil engineering, through the other engineering specialisms, chemistry, and physics, to biochemistry at the present day. The value of these bodies in the earliest days is clear—they performed a function, teaching and furthering their subject, which was on the whole being neglected by the universities, the only other centres for advanced education. This function has remained,

CONCLUSION

with the associations largely concerned with the particular,
practical application of the more theoretical sciences taught
by the universities, or even, since the universities do not cater
for sufficiently large number, by themselves through their
qualifying examinations.

The qualification function is obviously of great importance,
even if in some cases it is second to the technical study function.
Some of the later non-engineering associations were founded
mainly as qualifying bodies, and these show a greater resem-
blance to other professional bodies. Here again there are good
reasons why the association should follow an increased industrial
application of the study, for qualification is a means of guaranteeing the ability of an individual to a prospective employer and
of controlling the quality of those admitted into membership.
The associations dealt with in this study have a high degree
of control over new entrants, even though the universities
offer an alternative qualification, since many graduates also
seek Institution membership, but little control over the employment of their members. Qualification is clearly related to the
idea of status, since the reason for controlling the quality of
members is to maintain or enhance the status of the whole
group, assuming that ability will be given due financial and
other rewards.

Such is the preoccupation of the engineering Institutions in
particular with the technical study function that they show no
more concern with professional status than the upholding of the
standards of qualification. They make the assumption that
ability will be given its due reward. Some of the other associations, however, indicate by their activities that they believe that
this is not necessarily the case, and that some form of representation is needed. For the most part members are left to make
their own arrangements over their conditions of employment
with their employers, and such activities as the associations do
carry out are mainly intended to strengthen the individual
rather than to undertake any form of collective action. The
popular salary surveys are a good example of this; and the
fact that these seem to be welcome to many employers is an
indication also of the general attitude that prevails—that the
associations should co-operate with management as much for
the benefit of the latter and the economy as a whole as for the
association's members.

123

# CONCLUSION

These activities reflect the attitudes of the members themselves, which are clearly of a status type. Many of them want their association to concern itself with their problems of salary and status, but the means suggested for the most part involve no element of conflict with management, in whose ranks indeed a number of them are to be found. Suggestions such as more publicity, to educate the public in the value of scientists and engineers, and co-operative discussions with management are typical of an attitude which believes that where a man does not receive the 'due reward' for his ability, then this is a result of ignorance or misunderstanding, and should be remedied for the benefit of all. The 'due reward' is what a man should earn, not what he can fight for by collective bargaining.

Only a minority see any element of conflict in their relations with their employer, and even this is usually of a mild sort. Nevertheless, this attitude does indicate a change from the harmonious concept of status to the conflict concept of class, and is reflected in a desire that their association should undertake collective bargaining. A few of the associations do engage a little in activities of this sort, in those instances where a sizeable proportion of their members need and want collective bargaining. These people, the 'unprofessional professionals', are the most interesting in terms of the theoretical structure of this study. These, the least satisfied with their salaries and status and the most favourable towards collective bargaining, are to be found mainly amongst those employed by public corporations, the younger members, those less qualified, and those whose work is more technical than administrative. Such people tend towards attitudes of a class type, which are exemplified in trade unionism. It is, then, to this subject, to a consideration of those professional scientists and engineers who have actually joined a trade union, that the study now turns.

# Part III

# TRADE UNIONISM

# Introduction

Trade unionism, as explained in the second chapter, is understood as an expression of a class ideology, of the recognition of the need to bargain with an employer. In this section the first chapter is a survey of all the trade unions which have qualified scientists and engineers among their members. The extent of their membership, and the reasons for their success or failure, will be discussed. In the second chapter the question of trade unionism in private industry is considered in greater detail, by studying one particular union. This consideration is designed, firstly, to show how success in organization varies in different industries and between various groups because of differences in employment situation, and secondly, to demonstrate the attitudes of the members towards their union. The emphasis, therefore, is on trade unions as a class manifestation, but just as the influence of class attitudes within the professional associations was assessed, so equally is the effect of status ideas on trade unionism.

# CHAPTER SEVEN

# Trade Unions

---

There are a number of difficulties in the way of an assessment of the success of trade unionism amongst engineers and scientists, and it is virtually impossible to give precise and accurate data on the extent of unionization. The main reason is that many of the unions involved are not specifically unions of scientists and engineers; in some cases these form only a small proportion of their membership, and they do not therefore concern themselves in any special way with this group. Nor do they usually have specific information about their membership in it. Even where the union does recruit from this single field, there is still the problem of qualification. Qualified scientists and engineers are rigidly defined for the purpose of this study, but few trade unions are concerned with such niceties, and it becomes very difficult to separate the qualified from the others in membership statistics. Where there is selectivity it is usually in terms of grade or of the type of work performed rather than of academic qualifications. Whilst the two are very much related, they are not always so. Of two men doing exactly the same job, for example, one may be qualified and at the start of his career, the other unqualified and at the end.

These difficulties, however, do not prevent one saying anything at all. There is little reason to suppose that scientists and engineers are greatly different from others of similar status, for example the science teacher will be very much like his non-science colleagues, and the engineers in local government like other officers of comparable grade. The experience of these larger groups is probably also the experience of the particular sub-group. In other instances there may be lack of precision, but the general picture is reasonably clear.

The meaning of 'trade union' in this chapter, as in the whole study, needs to be made clear. As was pointed out in Chapter 2, the main factor, from the theoretical point of view, is taken to be the existence of bargaining relationships with management. Fortunately, since some bodies which would be included by this definition might see the name 'trade union' as a rather derogatory description of themselves, this is essentially the same view as that taken by the Ministry of Labour.[1] For reasons of convenience and clarity, it seems best to divide the unions dealt with in the following survey into three main areas: first, local and central government; second, nationalized industry; and third, private industry.

## CENTRAL AND LOCAL GOVERNMENT

In central government there is really only one union catering for scientists and engineers, the Institution of Professional Civil Servants. Founded in 1919, at about the same time as the Whitley Council for the Civil Service, the Institution has always tended to regard its 'Civil Service professional objectives as the most important',[2] and it is, according to another author, one of those organizations which 'are distinctly not unions and are distinctly out of line with union psychology'.[3] Nevertheless, he sees the Institution as 'one of the remarkable exploits in the history of organization . . . , whose membership, now exceeding eight thousand [in 1933], is drawn from persons by training and social background either indifferent or hostile to such a movement, and who as scientists are probably more individualistic than any other body of civil servants'.[4] Currently the membership of the Institution is well over fifty thousand, and its target figure of sixty thousand represents something very close

[1] Ministry of Labour, *Directory of Employers' Associations, Trade Unions, etc.* In this, unions are defined as 'all Associations of Employees, and Federations of such Associations, whether registered under the Trade Union Acts or not, known to the Department to include in their objects that of negotiating with employers with a view to regulating the wages and working conditions of their members'.
[2] E. N. Gladden, *Civil Service Staff Relationships*, William Hodge and Co., 1943, p. 82.
[3] L. D. White, *Whitley Councils in the British Civil Service*, University of Chicago Press, 1933, p. 273.
[4] Ibid., p. 271.

to the potential. Its recruitment must therefore be reckoned very successful, the evidence being that it is now relatively much more so than in 1933.[1] The Institution is not registered as a trade union, but, to judge from its Annual Reports, there can be little doubt that its prime concern is with the remuneration of its members. Notwithstanding the existence of the Civil Service Pay Research Unit, the I.P.C.S. runs its own Research Department, much of whose work is to collect and analyse material in connection with salary claims and to analyse the reports of the C.S.P.R.U. The concern with remuneration is even seen as a national duty–'Staff associations in the Civil Service have a responsibility not only to themselves and their members, but to the rest of the employed people in this country to see that the Government becomes an employer whose terms of employment at least command respect if they cannot command admiration.'[2] The higher levels of the Civil Service, nevertheless, do seem to maintain salaries comparable with those of other professional groups.[3]

Local government is dominated by one body to a far greater extent than is the Civil Service. The National and Local Government Officers Association claims to be the largest non-manual union in the world and the sixth largest union in Great Britain. Scientists and engineers, mostly the latter, form only a small proportion of the membership. This totals around 260,000, whereas the number of engineers employed in local government is only about seven thousand. Of these, some 80 per cent are probably members of N.A.L.G.O., an indication of the Association's success in recruiting. Because of their small numbers, the influence of engineers within N.A.L.G.O. can

---

[1] The total increase in the number of civil servants employed between 1933 and 1955 is 157·3 per cent. The largest increase, affecting scientists and engineers and civilian staffs in defence, is 356·6 per cent.

[2] Institution of Professional Civil Servants, *Annual Report 1959*, para. 19.

[3] However, there seems to be an unfavourable comparison between professional and administrative civil servants. The secretary of the I.P.C.S. has calculated that whereas the average career of the latter will yield a salary of £77,000, that of the former only £59,000 (S. Mayne, 'Incentives', Paper No. 14 in *The Direction of Research Establishments*–the Proceedings of a Symposium held at the National Physical Laboratory in September 1956, H.M.S.O., 1957). Some evidence of dissatisfaction with this situation can be found in N. Walker, *Morale in the Civil Service*, Edinburgh U.P., 1961, p. 245, and in the evidence of the I.P.C.S. to the Priestley Commission on the Civil Service.

only be very slight, although as has already been said they are probably very similar to other senior officers. The influence of the senior men as a whole seems to be greater than their numbers would suggest.[1]

N.A.L.G.O. was founded in 1905, but it was not until the end of the First World War that moves towards greater militancy were made.[2] Strong arguments were at that time put forward for registration as a trade union, but as a result of a ballot of members, certification was decided upon as an alternative. The Association is still not registered, but in recent years the main area of controversy has been not over this but over the question of affiliation to the T.U.C. A number of ballots, the most recent being held in 1962, have expressed opposition to such a move, though the majorities against have tended to shrink.[3] There seems little doubt that this opposition is greater among the higher grades, and it is strongly held. So strongly, in fact, that there is a possibility of large-scale resignations from the union should affiliation take place, particularly among the higher grades, including engineers. By creating this fear of weakening the Association, though not deliberately perhaps, this group is able to exercise a somewhat disproportionate influence. The situation is similar with regard to the use of strike action. The present rules require 90 per cent of a branch to vote in favour of such action before it can be carried out. So large a majority is hardly likely to be achieved without a radical change of attitude on the part of many members, but the requirement is a necessary one. Without it, many would fail to lend their support to the strike action, and a substantial number would probably resign.

Some local government engineers are dissatisfied with their position within N.A.L.G.O. They feel that they suffer from being an unimportant minority and that their interests are swamped by those of the lower clerical grades. This dissatisfaction has led to an attempt to obtain separate representation. Until 1947 this was to some extent provided by the Institution of Municipal and County Engineers, but in that year this body applied for a Royal Charter, which meant that it had to give up all activities usually dealt with by a trade union. The

[1] D. Lockwood, *The Blackcoated Worker*.
[2] An account of N.A.L.G.O. is given in Lockwood, op. cit., pp. 184–94.
[3] This decision was reversed in 1964.

engineers were unwilling to lose their representation and so in the same year was formed the Association of Local Government Engineers and Surveyors, still very closely connected with the Institution, to take over the work of looking after the interests of its members. It is open only to those who are professionally qualified or who are studying to become so, and its membership is about 3,300 out of an estimated potential of between seven and ten thousand. It is difficult to determine how many of these are also members of N.A.L.G.O., probably a high proportion, since A.L.G.E.S. does not see itself necessarily as an alternative. It recognizes the power that N.A.L.G.O. derives from its size and comprehensiveness, but it fears that engineers and others may become submerged. It believes that pressure 'can be brought to bear by the large number of non-professional officers from general division upwards to ensure that proposals by the National Executive Council are in their interests, without necessarily being fair or adequate for other classes of members'.[1] Largely, therefore, it acts as a sectional pressure-group on N.A.L.G.O., with which there is a large measure of co-operation, but it does also have some direct representation on the Joint Negotiating Committee for Chief Engineers. This tends to make it more attractive to senior engineers, the ones who might be less willing to join N.A.L.G.O., but it does also make it subject to the criticism of being a 'Chief Officers' Club'.

The position as regards teachers is very much more complex. It is impossible to separate scientists (there are few engineers) from the others, though it may well be unnecessary. The National Union of Teachers, which was founded in 1870 and now has some 220,000 members, is by far the largest body, but is probably of little importance for science teachers, who are mostly to be found in grammar schools. About one-third of all graduates in grammar schools are in the N.U.T.,[2] and most of the rest are probably members of either the Incorporated Association of Assistant Masters in Secondary Schools, founded in 1891, now with 23,000 members, or the Association of Assistant Mistresses in Secondary Schools. If scientists differ at all from their colleagues they are more likely to be union members, since their financial inferiority, when compared

[1] Association of Local Government Engineers and Surveyors, *A.L.G.E.S. Bulletin*, vol. 3, no. 1, April 1961, p. 4.
[2] A. Tropp, *The School Teachers*, Heinemann, 1957, p. 251 n.

with those in industry, is most marked. The shortage of scientists and mathematicians, however, has led to very few special concessions to this group. Many lecturers in technical and teacher training colleges are also members of the N.U.T., which has a system of joint membership with the Association of Teachers in Technical Institutions. The least like a trade union is the Association of University Teachers, but none of the bodies mentioned are registered. Only the N.U.T. has ever seriously contemplated strike action, though it has never actually carried it out. Such action would seem to be even more distasteful to the members of the other, more 'superior' bodies.

## NATIONALIZED INDUSTRIES AND PUBLIC CORPORATIONS

The development of a trade union for scientists and engineers in the coal industry is an interesting story. Before nationalization colliery officials were only weakly organized and they tended to identify themselves with their employers. There was a National Association of Colliery Managers, but this was mainly a technical society and strongly refuted any suggestions that it was a trade union. However, as Carr-Saunders and Wilson note, with some prescience, this attitude did not seem to originate from any inherent objection to collective action.[1] Nationalization soon led to moves to form a bargaining body. One trade union was even given help in its formation by the Yorkshire coal-owners who 'became concerned about the welfare of their staffs after nationalization',[2] but the N.A.C.M. and various professional bodies in 1947 sponsored the British Association of Colliery Management, now the major union for engineers and scientists in the industry. Its membership of 16,000 represents something like 95 per cent of its full potential. Most of these are mining and other engineers, and there are furthermore a number of scientists who are members of another union, the Association of Scientific Workers. The

[1] See Carr-Saunders and Wilson, *The Professions*, O.U.P., 1933, p. 154. Even before the war when nationalization was suggested, there was talk of changing the objects of the Association in order to include collective bargaining.
[2] B. MacCormick, 'Managerial Unionism in the Coal Industry', *B.J.S.*, vol. 11, 1960, p. 358. The article gives a good account of the B.A.C.M.

B.A.C.M. is registered as a trade union, but it is not affiliated to the T.U.C., since it considers this as a body identified with a political party that many of its members do not support. Although its policies on salaries, negotiating machinery and so on are little different from those of the mineworkers' union, there would probably be a much less favourable attitude towards strike action.

The electricity supply industry never underwent the same traumatic experience of nationalization as the coal industry. A good deal of it was formerly controlled by public bodies of one sort or another, so that the change did not radically affect the position of the staff. The main trade union, the Electrical Power Engineers' Association, was founded in 1913, and its part in collective bargaining machinery goes back to 1920. Its membership of 17,000 includes the great majority of those who are fully qualified, together with many who are not. The E.P.E.A. is a registered trade union, and it is affiliated to the T.U.C. Its formal 'objects' even include a reference to striking, though it is to 'discourage the use of the strike until other means of settling disputes have been explored'.[1] There are also two other bodies in electricity supply. The Association of Managerial Electrical Executive, as its name implies, caters more for managerial grades including non-engineers, whilst the Association of Supervisory Electrical Engineers, a rather smaller body which is a registered trade union, is not solely concerned with the electricity supply industry.

Three other nationalized industries employ a substantial number of scientists and engineers, most of whom are members of the appropriate trade union. Those in the U.K.A.E.A. are covered by the I.P.C.S. which has already been dealt with. Its A.E.A. branch has about 4,000 members, whilst there are only around 4,200 qualified scientists and engineers employed by the Authority. Even allowing for the probable wider base of membership of the I.P.C.S. there seems to be a very successful degree of recruitment. In the gas industry, because of its past close connections with local government, a number of employees are members of N.A.L.G.O. There are also two other bodies for staff employees, though neither of them caters solely for scientists and engineers. The main one is the Gas Officers Guild, with about 1,000 members, recruited from those who are pur-

[1] Electrical Power Engineers' Association, *Facts About the E.P.E.A.*, p. 5.

suing or training for a professional career, mainly engineers and chemists, but including also chartered secretaries, accountants and so on. It holds nine of the fifteen seats on the Senior Gas Officers Joint Council. As in the coal industry, nationalization was crucial. Before this, for senior staff 'the idea of a union was unthinkable, for the industry was a paternal one and officers were able reasonably satisfactorily to negotiate their own affairs'. Now however, 'it can be said of scientists and engineers in the gas industry that the majority have accepted the necessity for a trade union to safeguard their collective and individual interests'.[1] The older, long-service staff were much less willing to establish joint negotiating machinery than the younger, newer entrants, but the Guild claims that 'within two or three years of its foundation, between eighty per cent and ninety per cent of all "engineers and managers" in Great Britain, had joined it'.[2]

For engineers and scientists employed in the nationalized transport undertakings there are two trade unions. The first, and by far the largest, is the Transport Salaried Staffs Association, founded in 1897. This was registered as a trade union in 1899, and is affiliated to the T.U.C. It has a long record of militancy, having first undertaken strike action in 1919.[3] Within the T.S.S.A., however, such engineers as there are have little or no influence, and it is doubtful how far they favour this militancy. The British Transport Officers' Guild, though perhaps less effective, is likely to be more successful in recruiting such people. In view of their small numbers it is probable that a quite high proportion of engineers employed by British Railways and the other bodies are in a trade union.

## PRIVATE INDUSTRY

The position in private industry is quite different from that in central and local government and in the nationalized industries. Trade unionism has made a great deal of headway in the latter, but in the former is relatively unimportant. Nevertheless, since it is in private industry that the phenomenon

[1] In a personal communication from the Executive Chairman of the Gas Officers' Guild.

[2] G.O.G., *What it is, What it does.*

[3] Lockwood (op. cit., pp. 155–61) gives an account of the T.S.S.A.

of trade unionism, however weak, is most interesting, it is necessary to describe it in some detail.

One union has already been mentioned in connection with the electricity supply industry. This is the Association of Supervisory Electrical Engineers, which has some members within this industry but also a good number outside it. It was founded in 1914, and although a registered trade union, places a great deal of emphasis on its technical activities. It is probably unique in being a union in which owners and principals of business undertakings are admitted to membership. Some idea of its nature can be gained from the following statement, that 'in the field of representations on salaries and other conditions of employment, the A.S.E.E. specializes in conducting negotiations at high-level in a forceful yet non-militant manner, a method of procedure which does not jeopardize the existence of the all-important good relations between management and staff'.[1]

The British Association of Chemists, which says of itself that it is 'a Professional Association and is also a registered trade union', is another body of some importance. It was founded in 1917 'as a result of conditions which prevailed during the First World War, when chemists first entered industry on a large scale'.[2] Since that time it has grown steadily to its present membership of 2,000. Of this number about one-half are fully qualified, and most of these are employed in private industry. The B.A.C. therefore represents around 5 to 6 per cent of qualified chemists employed in industry. Perhaps because of this rather weak position, the Association does not conduct formal negotiations. Most of its work is in taking up the cases of particular members, mainly informally, but extending in some cases to legal aid. Its major concern with salaries is to publish minimum salary scales, which are widely used and recognized in the chemical industry. It also publishes an appointments circular, in which it tries to discourage members from applying for posts at salaries below those recommended by the B.A.C. for various qualifications. The Association is a politically neutral body, but it has important international links with similar European organizations for 'cadres', or professional and managerial workers.

[1] Association of Supervisory Electrical Engineers, *Year Book 1959–60*, p. 20.
[2] British Association of Chemists, *The British Chemist*, vol. xxx, Part 3, June 1958, p. 27.

# TRADE UNIONS

## ASSOCIATION OF SCIENTIFIC WORKERS

The Association of Scientific Workers has been chosen for special study. It is the largest trade union with members in private industry, though part of its membership is in fact drawn from various public organizations. It caters for all types of scientists and engineers throughout the range of private industry, but it is not limited only to those who are qualified. It has two sections of membership, the first for 'professionally competent scientists or engineers', the second for scientific or engineering workers under the supervision of the former. Approximately one-fifth of the Association's 17,000 members are in Section 1, but not all of these are fully qualified. A more detailed consideration of the qualifications of members is postponed to the next chapter.

The A.Sc.W. was originally founded in 1918 as the National Union of Scientific Workers, and was from the first registered as a trade union. It began with 500 members, all of them qualified, and its aims were to 'advance the interests of science pure and applied', and to 'regulate the relations between Scientific Workers and their employers'. Within four years membership had risen to 826, some 16 per cent of potential, estimated at 5,000. There followed a small but steady rise in membership until 1926, though the proportion of the potential actually fell. During this period there was a decline in militancy and radical feeling within the union, and the growing opposition to the idea of unionism combined with the failure of a recruiting campaign, blamed on the politics (Labour) of the General Secretary, finally culminated in deregistration in 1926 and a change of name to the present one. Resignations continued, however, mainly from those in industry, and as new bodies began to cater for several of the other groups of employees, numbers fell to 1,000 in 1930 and to 700 in 1935. This was the low-water mark. Interest began to revive, and was associated with a greater emphasis on trade-union rather than technical activities. In 1940 eligibility for membership was widened to include, in Section 2, the new types of lower-level technicians. At about this time, too, the Association was made aware of its weak legal position in negotiating a particular issue, and it was again registered as a trade union. Two years later it became affiliated to the T.U.C.

Membership now rose rapidly, from 2,000 in 1941 to 4,500 in 1942, and to 9,000 by 1943.

Throughout the rest of the war years and immediately after numbers continued to increase to a maximum of 15,500 in 1948. Even at this time, however, it was estimated that only 5 per cent of qualified potential members had been recruited. From then decline set in until the mid-fifties, after which membership remained fairly steady at around 12,000. The reasons for the decline are various. The A.Sc.W. itself believes it to be due largely to the change from war-time conditions: the disbandment of many large Government and private research establishments, the change to permanent status of many temporary civil servants, a scattering of scientists among many smaller firms, and a less co-operative attitude on the part of employers. To these should probably be added the change to a more favourable market situation for scientists and engineers, and a reversion to more middle-class attitudes on the part of many of them. Since 1960 membership has again risen.

The purpose of the A.Sc.W., according to its literature, is 'to improve the status and economic conditions of those engaged in scientific and technical work; and to promote the more effective use of science and scientific method for the welfare of society'. A certain amount is done in pursuance of this second object, but by far the greater emphasis is on the first. Included in the statements of immediate policy are such matters as a demand for straightforward increases in salaries, equal pay for women, minimum salary scales and regular increments, more favourable fringe benefits, protection in cases of unjust treatment, and for scientific work to be competently directed by properly qualified scientists. The Association describes itself as a 'protective professional organization, registered as a trade union', but it has few of the attributes of the former. Its technical activities are few, and it performs no qualifying function. Its main appeal, like that of most other trade unions, is realistically enough to self-interest.

Although a member of the T.U.C. the A.Sc.W. is not affiliated to the Labour Party. In 1959 the Annual Council asked the Executive Committee to prepare a report on affiliation, but no further action towards this end has been taken. There is a Political Fund, but it is used only for general lobbying activities to further the use of science and the interests of scientists. The Association is also prepared to help candidates of any party who are members or who will pay special attention to scientific affairs. Reference to the Political Fund is made periodically in the Journal, pointing out its purposes and emphasizing its non-party nature, but many members still seem to think of it as a payment to the Labour Party, while others perhaps think it is not worthwhile. In any case the Association makes it very easy indeed to contract out, and all but a tiny minority do so.

The Association has only fairly recently, in May 1962, under-gone its first experience of a full-scale strike. It arose from a request by the A.Sc.W. for a meeting with the management of a firm in the chemical industry to discuss the salaries of laboratory assistants, which was met with a refusal on the grounds that the company did not recognize trade unions for their staff. Two token one-hour stoppages by the branch members led to their indefinite suspension by the company, and a letter (described by the union as an ultimatum) asking the members to return to work under the present conditions or be dismissed. The Associa-tion thereupon declared an official strike, which continued for eight weeks until a compromise was eventually reached. The basic demand of the union, for official recognition, was conceded however. The incident, though minor in itself, provides some illumination of the situation in which the A.Sc.W. finds itself. The attitude of the employers towards a staff union is typical of many in the chemical industry in particular, but also of many others. A dispute over recognition was the sort to ensure maximum sympathy from other mem-bers, as is shown by the success of the strike fund, which was financed by the contributions from other branches. Finally, the workers in dispute were laboratory assistants, the younger and less qualified members who are probably the major concern of the A.Sc.W.

This first real example of strike action may well prove crucial for the Association. The major benefit may be to encourage more clear thinking on the subject of strikes on the part of both officials and ordinary members. Hitherto there has been a tendency for the Association to take an ambiguous, even ambivalent line. At the time of the one-day token stoppages in the engineering industry in 1962, for example, there was a good deal of debate as to whether or not the A.Sc.W. should take part as far as the appropriate branches were concerned. The only lead that these branches were given from head office was that members were asked not to undertake any work normally done by the strikers and not to force their way through the picket lines. The decision on whether or not to strike was left to the branches. There was some feeling that a much clearer lead should have been given on a question of such importance, and that the matter of not crossing a picket line showed an ambiguity. The difficulty of course is that branches differ a good deal in their composition and nature, particularly in the proportion of 'moderates' and 'militants'. To avoid offence to either, but especially the former, the central officials can pass such problems on to the branches, but unfortunately the difficulties are not much less for the latter. Each branch still has to be wary of offending its own moderates.

This policy of leaving decisions to be made by the branches themselves is not wholly a matter of shirking of responsibility by the central officials. There is also in the A.Sc.W. a positive policy of delegation and of allowing the branches the greatest possible autonomy. This stems from a desire on the part of the great majority of members for a union which is responsible in both senses of the word.[1] The strength of the belief in democratic decentralization is indicated by the fact that attendance at ordinary branch meetings is around 25 to 30 per cent. Often, however, the members who demand the most 'moderation' are not the ones who attend meetings, so that many issues are put to a referendum in the branch.

## Nature of Professional Unionism

The foregoing survey of trade unions for scientists and engineers has shown wide variations in their nature. They range from bodies in which technologists form only a small minority to those which are restricted to the qualified, and from unions whose members are in just one industry to those where they are widely spread. Nevertheless, despite the diffi-

[1] A 'meticulous attention to democratic form' is also noted in some American trade unions. Here it may interfere with bargaining procedure, preventing the union representatives from speaking with full authority. See R. E. Walton, *The Impact of the Professional Engineering Union*, Harvard University, 1961, p. 38.

culties which these variations present, it is possible and useful to make some generalizations about the nature of trade unionism amongst scientists and engineers.

The names of the different bodies provide a first clue to their nature. Most of them are called an 'Association', a few a 'Guild' or an 'Institution', and with the exception of the teachers not one is called a 'Union'. This may appear superficial, but it does indicate the reluctance of these bodies to see themselves as trade unions. Only six are registered under the Trade Union Act, and all of them, apart from the T.S.S.A., are among the smaller associations. Even where an organization has taken advantage of the legal benefits of registration this is no indication that it thereby recognizes itself as a body similar to other trade unions, especially those of the manual workers. Only three of the associations, including the rather special T.S.S.A., are affiliated to the T.U.C. There does not even seem to be a great deal of common feeling amongst themselves, or if it exists, it has not yet found concrete expression. There is a National Federation of Professional Workers, which is sometimes inaccurately described as 'the white-collar T.U.C.', but only three of the associations are members, and two of these are affiliated to the T.U.C. in any case. The general reluctance to join the N.F.P.W. is probably due less to the ideological objections which prevent affiliation to the T.U.C. than to doubts about its usefulness. Opposition to the idea of joining the T.U.C. certainly is ideological. At least some of the organizations, even some of those not registered, have accepted the fact that they are trade unions and that they are therefore very much like other, even manual workers' trade unions. Many members, more or less grudgingly, have also accepted the fact, but would not accept membership of the T.U.C. because of the political implications that they see in this. The same sort of objections are found even when the union is affiliated to the T.U.C., for then the argument is made that this does not really hold any political implications. There is then a similar opposition to affiliation to the Labour Party. Only the T.S.S.A. is in fact affiliated. The Political Fund which a few of these unions have is used solely for non-party purposes.

These facts support Wright Mills' observations about white-collar unions in general in the United States, that 'there is undoubtedly more principled rejection than principled acceptance of the unions. Pro-union ideology serves primarily to clear away principled objections in order that an instrumental view may come to the fore. . . . Unions are usually accepted as something to be used rather than something in which to believe.'[1] This distinction between the principled and instrumental acceptance of unions is well exemplified in the situation that has just been described. Many scientists and engineers are prepared to join bodies which are, literally in all but name, trade unions, but their membership is not always wholehearted. They are not necessarily apathetic, except perhaps when it comes to taking office, but their insistence on democratic procedure is mainly to ensure 'moderation'. Registration, affiliation to the T.U.C. and affiliation to the Labour Party are each in turn opposed on political, ideological and principled grounds.

Scientists and engineers not only see their unions as instrumental, they see them as different types of instruments from those of the manual workers. In part this is a result of the attitudes of the members towards the union itself, the great emphasis on democracy which has already been mentioned. More important, however, is the attitude towards management, which is the positive aspect of the negative rejection of the principles of unionism. The ideology of these groups is on the whole favourable to management, and even where they have accepted the instrumental value of a union it is usually only with reluctance. Some see unionism as undesirable but inevitable, others as only necessary because management has forced it upon them by its 'aberrations'. They feel that they are not treated as they deserve and that this is undesirable for the whole of society as well as for themselves. They see, or rationalize, their own interests as the interests of all, and their attitude towards collective bargaining is essentially one of helping management to see reason—to preserve it from its own follies.[2]

[1] C. Wright Mills, *White Collar*, Oxford U.P., 1956, p. 308. As Mills himself says, the difference between the blue- and white-collar worker is not very great in this respect. Even in Britain it would be rash to assume a widespread principled 'belief in' unions amongst manual workers. The ideology of the union officials, combined with what the members are prepared to accept, seems more important.

[2] Walton (op. cit., p. 25) paraphrases the typical approach of many professional engineering unions thus: 'We have certain needs, and these are reasonable needs; therefore, all we have to do is educate management re-

There is thus a great emphasis on co-operation, which finds its expression in the official objects of the associations as well as in the attitudes of the members. These show a high degree of responsibility: 'the Guild acts on the principle that one of its important functions is to promote the smooth running of the industry';[1] 'to foster co-operation between employers and employees in the common interest';[2] 'to promote the general advancement and efficiency of the means of production, transmission, distribution and utilization of electricity'.[3]

A major indication of this pro-management feeling is the attitude towards strike action. On this criterion one might describe the A.Sc.W. as the most militant of the unions under consideration, but this would be solely on its record of one small strike over recognition. Of the others only a few have even considered the possibility of striking, and these have so far rejected it. There is a good deal in the argument that for many categories of technologist the strike weapon is impracticable. To put it lightly, no one would notice that they were not at work, at least for some time. In this sense their power position is weak. It is even weaker, of course, in the case of those unions whose members are in private industry, where representation is often of only a minority. This weakness can also be used to explain the lack of militancy in bargaining. In the extreme case, as with the B.A.C. and some branches of the A.Sc.W., there is no real bargaining at all, but some form of occasional representation.

This weakness is not the whole explanation, however. There are the examples of the unions in government and the nationalized industries where representation is high, which are still very much against strike action. The main reason must be ideological, a desire not to prejudice their pro-management attitude. This does often mean that a minority of members, or even non-members, can exercise a disproportionate influence. The union has the problem of trying to attract new members and of retaining its marginal supporters, which means trying to pursue a moderate course. Thus in any discussion of strike action, for example, or N.A.L.G.O.'s perennial problem of

garding our problems; being comprised of reasonable men management will set about to solve the problems.' This, however, he sees as an 'early relationship', before the onset of disillusionment. On this see also p. 37.

[1] G.O.G., op. cit.      [2] A.S.E.E., introductory leaflet.
[3] E.P.E.A., op. cit., p. 4.

affiliation to the T.U.C., many members will take a moderate stand, not out of principle but out of a desire to conciliate the moderates.

Certain other services are provided by most of these unions which, partly because of the lesser emphasis on collective bargaining but also because of the different work and needs of technologists, are of relatively greater importance than in manual workers' unions. One example is legal protection, which covers not only claims against an employer in the event of injury, but also in the case of a member becoming legally liable as a result of some action at work or of a dispute over a contract of employment. There is also much evidence of the professional nature of this group, in the emphasis given to technical education by many of the unions, and in the more direct concern with professional matters, for example the object of the G.O.G. 'to maintain the highest standard of professional conduct by members',[1] or that of the E.P.E.A. 'to secure legal certification of qualified engineers and to support the principle that such engineers should be members of a recognized protective association'.[2] Most of the associations also have an unemployment benefit scheme, and many an appointments bureau. Perhaps of little theoretical importance, but an attractive feature to a number of potential members, are the various schemes for cheaper insurance, mortgages and discount trading, which some of the unions offer. They do not serve to overcome the principled objection to unionism but the fairly common practical objection that a union can be of no real benefit. Some individuals can be persuaded that their savings under these schemes will be greater than the union subscription.

It is obvious from what has already been said that unions for scientists and engineers differ in several ways from those of manual workers. In dealing with a similar group of American unions, Goldstein[3] suggests that theirs is 'a form of trade unionism that differs significantly from traditional trade unionism' and that the differences are in four main relationships, between (1) salaried professionals and management, (2) salaried professionals and their unions, (3) the professional union and management, and (4) professional unions and the labour

[1] G.O.G., op. cit.    [2] E.P.E.A., op. cit., p. 5.
[3] B. Goldstein, 'Some Aspects of the Nature of Unionism among Salaried Professionals in Industry', *A.S.R.*, vol. 20, no. 2, April 1955, pp. 199–205.

movement. The first relationship is 'the basic one, the one that determines whether or not there is to be union organization'. This relationship with management is, in the terms of the present thesis, a function of the employee's ideology, his consciousness of status on the one hand or of class on the other. It is clear that for this group of employees there is still a great deal of status consciousness; their attitude is still in large part pro-management. The more true this is, however, the more important is the fact that individuals have joined a union, for the pressure of circumstances must have been that much greater. As has been seen, these status attitudes have been carried over into the trade union, to some extent influencing its activities, but the fact remains that this body is a trade union, its major function being to negotiate collectively with employers. These professional unions are different from those of the manual workers, but the similarities are nevertheless greater than the differences. The latter are explained by the different employment situation in which scientists and engineers are placed, and it is highly debatable, in view of the way in which employment situation can change, whether this form of trade unionism is significantly different from others. Trade unionism differs even amongst manual workers, certainly in different countries and at different times. There would seem to be, for example, a close parallel between the professional trade unions and the New Model unions of craftsmen in the mid-nineteenth century.[1] The existence of unionism amongst this group is of greater significance than are the present differences with 'traditional' trade unionism.

## TRADE UNION MEMBERSHIP

So far this general discussion has concerned itself only with the nature of the professional trade unions. An equally, or more important question is that of the relative success or failure of

[1] See, for example, R. W. Postgate, *The Builders' History*, Labour Publishing Co. ('It was a revolt in favour of caution, of care and method, of self-restraint and laborious attention to detail. The new generation was a servile generation' (p. 182)), and H. J. Fyrth and H. Collins, *The Foundry Workers*, A.U.F.W., 1959 ('We are desirous to be at peace with capital; the two interests capital and labour should work harmoniously together, for they cannot otherwise succeed'—Daniel Guile, General Secretary of the Friendly Society of Iron Founders in 1880, quoted on p. 40).

unionism in different areas, which gives a clue to the conditions under which unionism is likely to arise. This aspect will be pursued in more detail in the following chapter when a single trade union will be considered, but some general observations can be made here.

One fact emerges very clearly from the descriptions of the various associations which was presented earlier, that the great majority of them are to be found in government, both central and local, and in the nationalized industries. In these fields a very high proportion of scientists and engineers are organized, whereas in private industry only a small minority are in a union. To some extent this may be explained by differences in work situation, taking this in a wide sense. Most important in this respect is the far greater degree of bureaucratization in government and public bodies. The hierarchic organization is much more specifically defined, often more extensive and perhaps more centralized. Positions and offices are graded and ranked, salary levels are carefully and rationally assigned, and promotion is more systematic and predictable. These factors are very important, for their total effect is to transform the employee, and his image of himself, from an individual to a member of a work group. The relationship of his own to other offices is a well-defined one, and the emphasis is on the role rather than on the individual occupant. An employee's salary is not a confidential matter between himself and his employer, but a function purely of his grade. Since he cannot, within the same grade, substantially raise his salary, his interests are now, like those of his fellow employees, to raise the whole salary scale. This is even more true when, with the bureaucratic emphasis on academic qualifications, promotion is seen to have definite limits. Within an extensive and centralized hierarchy, power and authority are more difficult to locate in known individuals, and final authority may reside in some remote office with no possibility of personal contact.

This association of unionization with bureaucratization is noted by Lockwood,[1] who stresses the difference between the latter and 'administrative particularism'. This is a combination of bureaucracy with paternalism, which involves a lack of uniformity in working conditions, a personal relationship between employer and employee, confidentiality about salary

[1] Lockwood, op. cit., pp. 141–9.

and vagueness about promotion. These conditions are to be found within an ostensibly bureaucratic organization, and between the extremes of paternalism and bureaucracy there can be a number of intermediate stages. Government and the nationalized industries tend to be nearer the extreme of bureaucracy, whilst private industry is nearer to paternalism. Part of the explanation for this is that the former are larger and more highly centralized. There are, however, some very large and highly centralized private companies and some with a near-monopolistic position, in which administrative particularism is nevertheless much in evidence, and union organization very weak. This does not seem to be related to differing work content, for this may well be substantially the same in private as in nationalized industry, or the same industry—e.g. coal—before and after nationalization. Nor is it, as Croner[1] argues, that certain types of work are delegated managerial functions, an argument which is anyway difficult to uphold in the case of engineers and scientists.

The major reason for the difference is an ideological one. In government, and to a slightly lesser extent in the nationalized industries, there is not the same obvious and sharp division of interest between employers and employed; indeed the former may often be hard to define. Consequently there is not here the same objection to unionism. In the nationalized industries, of course, it was actually encouraged. Not only does bureaucracy, because of the conditions it imposes, encourage unionism, it requires it in order to make the determination of salaries and conditions truly impersonal. Since unions themselves need this collective impersonality, the two reinforce one another. Such conditions will lead to what has been called 'administrative' rather than 'protest' unionism.

In private industry, on the other hand, full bureaucratization is much less likely to come about, because of the need of the employers to ensure the co-operation of 'staff' employees, to retain their loyalty to management and to prevent the growth of a feeling of conflict of interest. This need, of course, has its negative aspect in the very forceful discouragement of unionism by some managements. The cumulative, reciprocal relationship between bureaucracy and unionism also has a negative side, in

[1] F. Croner, 'Salaried Employees in Modern Society', *International Labour Review*, vol. 69, no. 2, Feb. 1954, pp. 98–110.

that the absence of a union entails at least a certain degree of administrative particularism, and thus a situation which is less favourable to the development of unionism.

The ideological and 'political'[1] climate of an organization is important, but difficult to assess. There can be little doubt that given similar work conditions unionism will flourish where it is encouraged more than where it is opposed. On the other hand it is obvious that unions have developed in the face of strong opposition from employers. Again, for the group with which this study is concerned, there do exist unions in private industry, which are stronger in some areas than in others. Therefore, to avoid the problems involved in considering public employment, it seems best to examine the situation in private industry alone, and this we shall do in the next chapter.

[1] The situation described seems to be covered by Dahrendorf's idea of the political factors which affect class organization, as described in Chapter 2.

# CHAPTER EIGHT

# Trade Unionists

The aim of this chapter is to consider in greater detail one particular trade union and its members. The Association of Scientific Workers has already been briefly described, and something said of its history, aims and objects, nature and membership. A detailed consideration, however, can obviously yield a good deal more, and it was therefore decided to make a study of the A.Sc.W. at the local level, in this case the Merseyside area. This entails first of all a description of the branches—the industries in which they are found, their strength, and the reasons for it; and secondly a study of the members themselves and of the attitudes of these professional trade unionists. It may be that this concentration on one small area will tend to lessen the representativeness of the results, and this fact should be borne in mind. Nevertheless, the local study can be most fruitful, and it is unlikely that the general conclusions will fail to apply to some degree elsewhere.

## RECRUITMENT IN THE NORTH-WEST REGION

Before passing on to this local study, however, there is some more general material which can be presented. This has been obtained from an analysis of membership application forms for the North-West Region from 1955 to 1960. The information to be obtained from these forms is necessarily rather limited, but it will serve as a preliminary introduction.

Only applicants for Section 1 membership employed in private industry have been considered. In the five-year period there were 292 of these, just under one-half of whom (136) were fully qualified. Two-thirds of the remainder had fairly advanced technical qualifications. This does not necessarily mean that the former are in positions superior to the latter. It can happen that a qualified individual may be working with, or even subordinate to one completely unqualified except by experience. The former, of course, is likely to be younger and at the start of his career. However, since academic qualifications afford the only satisfactory criterion by which the group being studied can be defined, it is mainly with those who hold them that the study deals.

Even with a knowledge of the qualifications of these Section 1 members it is still very difficult to make an assessment of the strength of the A.Sc.W. in private industry. Approximately one-fifth of the total members are in Section 1, and one-third are fully qualified, four-fifths of them being employed in private industry. This gives a total of around 600—at best only 1 per cent of the 70,000 scientists and engineers employed in private industry. Its strength among those with lower qualifications is almost certainly higher, and it is in itself significant that the A.Sc.W. is becoming increasingly dominated by the less qualified.[1]

The present concern is not so much with the total strength of the A.Sc.W. as with its representation in different industries and among different groups of workers. Table 1 shows the recruitment of Section 1 members by industry in the North-West Region. One large group, the C.W.S. employees, are best left out of the discussion, since this employer is rather exceptional in encouraging its workers to become union members. With the exception of this group, the great majority are employed in the two main industries of electrical engineering and chemicals. This is to some extent to be expected, since these are the two major employers, but it is rather surprising that the others, mechanical engineering and aircraft, for example, are so poorly represented. In the absence of any detailed knowledge of the situation for scientists and engineers in these industries this is difficult to explain. Further study would probably show a different employment position from that in chemicals and engineering, almost certainly a far higher chance of obtaining

---

[1] For example, between 1949 and 1959 the proportion of Section 1 recruits to the total has fallen from 28 per cent to 18 per cent. A similar process of dilution may be going on within Section 1, but there is no real evidence of this.

## TABLE I

*Recruitment of Section 1 Members by Industry*
*(North-West Region, 1955–60)*

|  | Qualified | Semi-Qualified | Unqualified | Total |
|---|---|---|---|---|
| Electrical Engineering | 61 | 58 | 33 | 152 |
| C.W.S. | 35 | 6 | 1 | 42 |
| Chemicals | 22 | 17 | 6 | 45 |
| Engineering | 1 | 2 | 8 | 11 |
| Metals | 3 | 7 | 1 | 11 |
| Glass | 1 | 6 | 3 | 10 |
| Food | 5 | 2 | 2 | 9 |
| I.R.A.s | 6 | 1 | — | 7 |
| Paper, etc. | — | 2 | 1 | 3 |
| Textiles | 2 | — | — | 2 |
| Total | 136 | 101 | 55 | 292 |

promotion to management. A comparison between the two industries shows the importance of the work situation. It is not easy to be precise, but whereas the degree of unionization in the first, chemicals, is only around 1 per cent, in the other, electrical engineering, it is about 2·5 per cent. It is unlikely that the explanation for this lies in any particular feature of the North-West. If anything, one would expect to find more members from the chemical industry in this area. (It might be thought necessary to take the B.A.C. into account, since it has a higher representation in the chemical industry than the A.Sc.W. However, it is important to remember that this is a union which likes to stress that it is also a professional organization, and which does not engage in outright collective bargaining. Its existence does not really negate the argument being made.) A much better explanation lies in the differences in the type of work performed. Of the 24 new members from the chemical industry, 21 are in research and development work and 3 in process control. Of those from electrical engineering, nearly a half are employed in estimating for and preparing contracts, 10 are engaged in actual production, and 7 in testing. Thirteen are doing research and development, and 1 is in management. Apart from the one exceptional individual, all the members are, as the hypothesis requires, separated from the exercise of authority. They are part of the class to whom orders are given rather than of that which gives them. In both industries, one easily identifiable group of the former class, those engaged in research and development, constitute a substantial proportion of the membership. In electrical engineering, however, another group, whose work is closer to that of production, seem to be more highly unionized. The large group of contracts engineers, for example, are performing work which demands a high degree of skill and advanced qualifications, yet which is at the same time almost production work. This situation is fairly common in the electrical engineering industry,[1] especially on the electronics side, but there seem to be few parallels elsewhere. Many chemical processes require quality control, a technical function which is ancillary to production, but the techniques involved are usually straightforward and routine, and the work can be done by lesser qualified personnel. In most industries where mechanical engineers are employed there does not seem to be anything comparable. Many of these are, in fact, employed in management positions.

The difference between research and development and work of the sort which is close to production is obviously a vital one, in showing that a class ideology, and hence unionization, depends not only on being in a position of subordination, but in one in which this fact is emphasized. Both groups are in the same objective situation, but their total employment experience leads to differing subjective realization. The differences in employment experience are fairly obvious. The research worker has a much greater degree of personal control over his work. Although it is rare in industry for the researcher to be entirely his own master, nevertheless, given a general directive, the day-to-day control is his own. His output is not a clearly measurable quantity, nor, at least in the short run, can its quality be judged. The work itself also has an intrinsic technical interest, and, for the qualified worker, is much less of a routine. The work group, even in large organizations, is likely to be small, and although there is an authority structure within a research laboratory, it is not the sort to create divisions. The leader

[1] The only major American study of a professional engineering union was, significantly, of the Council of Western Electric Professional Employees. The Western Electric Co. manufactures telephone equipment for the Bell Telephone Co. See B. Goldstein, *Unions for Technical Professionals: a Case Study*, unpublished Ph.D. thesis, Chicago, 1957.

usually remains part of the work group, his authority derives largely from his superior technical ability and is thus highly legitimized. His identification remains much more with the research department than with management.[1]

For those workers engaged in production, or in work ancillary to it, the situation is very different. Their work is much more highly routinized, they will be gathered together in large work groups, their control over their work is much less, their output is much more easily measurable, and because of this they are more likely to be subject to pressure from management. Under these conditions they are more obviously separated from the exercise of authority, and unionization becomes more likely. Other factors serve to strengthen this tendency. Since this work is closely allied to production it is the sort to which some unqualified manual workers may be promoted. This contrasts in two ways with the situation in a research department. Just as the latter is physically distinct from production, so also is it socially distinct—promotion to it from elsewhere is rare, because the skills needed are very different from those used in production. With the other type of work there are both physical and social connections. This fact makes a feeling of association with production much more likely, and will tend to break down the feeling of apartness from the manual workers. An important result of this is a far greater acquaintance with trade unionism. These qualified engineers may not like all the activities of the manual workers' unions which they are now more able to observe, but they are faced with the contrast between their own weakness and the strength of the unions, with the benefits that they obtain from it. At the same time they will be working close to other employees who, as craftsmen, have been members of a strongly organized union. Some of those qualified will have had their own experience of trade-union membership, since a fairly common route to qualification in electrical engineering is through the drawing office in which there is already a high degree of unionization.[2]

[1] The research laboratory is not without its difficulties, however. See, for example, S. Marcson, *The Scientist in American Industry*, Harper, 1960; and W. Kornhauser, *Scientists in Industry*, California Press, 1962.

[2] The official historian of the Association of Engineering and Shipbuilding Draughtsmen (now the Draughtsmen and Allied Technicians Association) states that 'the A.E.S.D. has been able to organize approximately three out

In fact, 28 per cent of the recruits from this industry had previously been members of a union, as compared with only 9 per cent in chemicals. (For the semi-qualified group these proportions rise to 50 and 18 per cent respectively.) Trade-union organization at all levels is stronger in the engineering industry, and since the wage and procedural agreements affect many of the semi-qualified and a few of the qualified, the encouragement to join a union is that much greater.

## MERSEYSIDE BRANCHES

The strength of the A.Sc.W. in the electrical engineering industry is reflected in the size and nature of the branches on Merseyside. There are five with members in private industry. Two of them are single-firm branches in electrical engineering; one a geographically-based branch serving several firms in the chemical industry, with one major company predominating; one a single-firm branch in glass-making; and a general branch composed of Merseyside members not in any of the others.

Branch A has its members in a large company manufacturing telephone equipment, a very good example of an industry which employs qualified workers on semi-production tasks. It has 250 members out of an estimated potential of about 500, nearly one-half of whom are in Section 1. This success in the degree of organization has occurred only recently, following the takeover of the company by a larger group. This event seems to have been crucial. Previously the branch had been weakly organized and of little importance, but as a result of the takeover many of those who had formerly rejected the union 'on principle' now decided to join. A large number did so even before any of the policies of the new top management could take effect, mainly because of the insecurity that they now felt. The local top management, whom they knew and could identify themselves with, were replaced by an unknown, formal and centralized authority. Still more joined when it became apparent that their new employers were determined to put an end to the laxity of the past and to make economies. A rumour of

of every four engineering and shipbuilding draughtsmen' (J. E. Mortimer, *A History of the Association of Engineering and Shipbuilding Draughtsmen*, A.E.S.D., 1960, p. 413). The story of unionization amongst draughtsmen makes an interesting comparison with the situation of scientists and engineers.

redundancy, an exaggerated version of the truth, led to a good deal of union activity and some acrimonious feeling.

The branch officials took full advantage of this situation, which at last provided the union with a *raison d'être*. Formerly it had been weak, either because it was thought to have no purpose, or because it was thought to have no power. Having demonstrated that it had the former it was able to obtain the latter. The officials made constant representations to management, whose attitude during this period changed from one of scarcely veiled opposition to one of reluctant acceptance. The branch was quite successful, for example, in obtaining reasonable redundancy payments for those laid off. Another interesting fact is that during this period the A.Sc.W. entered into co-operative relationships with the other staff unions and even made some contacts with those of the manual workers.

This apparent militancy, however, is relative. Even in the fairly heated atmosphere of the meeting called to discuss the redundancy rumour, which was attended by about one-third of the members, the main motion passed was one asking members to publicize the problem in the newspapers (local and national 'quality') and to write to their M.P.s. There was also a motion passed banning overtime, but it seemed to be supported mostly by those who were never asked to work it. The final motion is a good example of the readiness to go beyond the branch meetings to the whole membership. This was to hold a ballot on the possibility of a protracted strike. The chances of a majority in favour were very poor—for example, a ballot held a short while earlier to decide whether or not to support the one-day token stoppage of the manual workers' unions in the engineering industry had been defeated by a majority of 129 to 66.

Altogether this is the most active and successful branch on Merseyside, though to what extent this is a result of the particular conditions at the time of the study is difficult to say. It is most probable that having established a definite relationship with the management, and having proved to its members that it can be of some benefit to them, the branch will continue to thrive.

Branch B is in a relatively small plant owned by a large electrical engineering company. This plant is new and the production process complex. Most of the qualified employees are physicists, chemists and metallurgists rather than electrical engineers, and since there is no research and development department their work is in actual production, quality control or maintenance. Though not as large as the first branch this one is, if anything, more successful in its recruiting–it has 61 members out of an estimated potential of a hundred. One-third of them are in Section 1.

The management, while not welcoming the A.Sc.W., has accorded its recognition and has from the start been reasonably co-operative. Mostly through the efforts of the A.Sc.W. all the staff unions are represented at regular monthly meetings, where individual and group grievances are discussed. The emphasis on both sides seems to be on consultation and co-operation.

Attendance at branch meetings is quite good, about one-quarter, with perhaps a greater interest from the more qualified members. In fact, the branch committee is made up almost entirely of these. This, however, should not be interpreted as a sign of greater militancy on their part. It is probably more a result of their desire to ensure the 'responsibility' of the branch.

Branch C is geographically based, but caters only for the employees of several local chemical firms. The great majority of members are from one major company. Before 1953 it was actually a branch of the Union of Shop, Distributive and Allied Workers, catering almost entirely for non-qualified laboratory assistants, but in that year the whole branch transferred to the A.Sc.W. Its situation offers an interesting contrast to that of the two already discussed. Not only does the branch cover a number of different companies, but the major company is itself split into a number of widely separated departments. There is therefore little chance of contact between members during working hours. The difficulty of collecting subscriptions means that members are encouraged to pay by bankers' order, but this prevents even the minimal degree of organization otherwise involved in this job. The extent of membership in the different departments varies considerably, and seems to rise and fall according to the influence of particular personalities. Branch meetings do not provide a satisfactory alternative way of unifying the members, since attendance is usually of the order of only 15 per cent.

As might be expected from the above the power of the branch is limited. Its 65 members are only a small proportion of the potential (apparently not even known), and there is no local negotiation with the managements. The major company has promised recognition if the union can obtain a 50 per cent membership. The only occasion on which the branch secretary sent a letter to this management he was given informal advice about his promotion prospects by the works manager. The main function of the A.Sc.W. seems to be in providing its general services and legal representation. One possible sign of apprehension on the part of the management is the recent institution of a system of staff committees on which anything, with the exception of salaries and individual cases, can be discussed. The wide variety of employees represented, however, prevents discussion of any but the most general issues.

Branch D has just recently been formed out of the general branch, so that little can be said about it. It has only about 15 members, employed in a large glass-making company. There has been an A.Sc.W. branch at this company before, around 1950, but enthusiasm waned. Now there has been a revival in interest which may perhaps survive.

The final branch, E, is a general branch whose members are recruited from any company where there are too few of them to form a separate branch. As one would expect, it is even more amorphous than Branch C, with very little contact between members, and little enthusiasm for branch meetings. It is, in fact, impossible to find a secretary from among their numbers, and this job has to be done by a member of another branch. The only benefits to the members are the general services provided by the union.

The five branches discussed show the wide variety of the membership of the A.Sc.W. By far the most successful in terms of recruitment and activity are the two in the electrical engineering industry. At the other extreme, the general branch is obviously the least active, and, as a branch, is virtually useless. The nature of the differences between the branches are best borne in mind in the following account of the members themselves, since related to them are differences in the attitudes of these members.

## A.Sc.W. Members

The material for this part of the study was obtained from interviews of 49 members of the A.Sc.W. living in the Merseyside area (there were 3 refusals). They are taken from the five branches described, and include all the fully qualified members (28) together with a sample of those with H.N.C. in order to allow reasonably large numbers to be dealt with. The latter group do not seem to be very much different from the former. The numbers from the five branches are: A 19, B and C 9, D 4, and E 8. Further details are given in the Appendix.

As one would expect, the great majority of the members are engaged in technical work. Twenty-eight are in wholly technical jobs and 9 in mainly technical ones. Only 8 are doing work which is mainly administrative, 4 of them being in Branch C and members of long standing.

Unfortunately, the limited situation being considered here does not produce sufficient evidence to support the hypothesis that those nearest to production are the ones most likely to unionize. Branch B does provide some, since 7 of its 9 members are engaged either in production or in process control, and it is the most successfully organized. In Branch A, the largest, however, most of the qualified members are doing research and development. This should not be taken as contrary evidence. In the first place, it probably means that this particular company uses qualified men much less in direct production work. Secondly, in this field it is not always easy to draw a line between development and design work, and the conditions under which the former is carried out differ greatly from those of the research ideal.

Most of the respondents (41) had had a grammar school education, but two-thirds had followed it only with part-time study. Those in Branch A had had the least formal education. None had been to university, and only 3 had had full-time education after leaving school. Eleven of the 19 had left school by the age of 16. Since we may well take this as evidence of lower social origins, it would seem that the type of work which is more likely to encourage unionization is in fact being performed by those whose background might anyway make them look more favourably on unions.[1] These individuals may have

---

[1] As J. A. Banks has said, 'The old manual working class is a shrinking class, relatively speaking; some of its children must move into clerical and technical jobs. In so far as these carry with them connotations of the occupations of "gentlemen", and so long as manual occupations continue to carry connotations of degradation, such children will move socially even if they

obtained the necessary academic qualifications, but their social origins, their method of training and their work may combine to prevent their full membership of the professional group. Members of the other branches for the most part have had a longer schooling, but with the exception of those in the general branch, the majority had only part-time further education. Taking the fully qualified alone, however, these were much more likely to have had full-time higher education. In the general branch 4 of the 6, and in Branch C 3 of the 4 qualified members had attended university. Considering just the fully qualified group, they do not appear to be less educated than is general throughout the respective professional groups.

A further idea of the differences between the branches can be had by looking at the age of the members and the year in which they joined. The two most successful branches are the ones with the most recent recruits. All but two of the members in Branches A and B have joined since 1960. On the other hand only one member of the general branch has joined since 1950. The other two branches are also composed of fairly long-standing members. It is not surprising, then, that Branches A and B are made up largely of young members (12 of the 19 in Branch A and 7 of the 9 in Branch B were born after 1930), whilst all the members of Branches D and E and the majority of those of Branch C were born before 1930. There would seem to have been a failure in recruitment by these latter branches, which indeed is not surprising in view of their general inactivity. Their members, however, do show a high degree of loyalty in continuing to pay their subscriptions without seeing much return. The two electrical engineering branches have obviously been more successful, but it is very difficult to say whether their newer membership is a sign of increasing unionization in this area, or just that they are mushroom growths which may die away when the particular conditions in their companies change.

This possibility seems greatest for Branch A where the conditions of the takeover precipitated the strong union organization. In fact, 13 of the 19 members give the takeover, or one or other aspect of it, as their reason for joining the A.Sc.W. (Table 2). Such an event, with its catalytic effect, is undoubtedly

merely take over ways of earning their living which are no longer followed in the main by children of clerks and technicians' (J. A. Banks, 'Moving Up in Society', *Twentieth Century*, May 1960, pp. 425–6).

# TRADE UNIONISTS

## TABLE 2

### *Reason for Joining*

| Branch | A | B | C | D | E | Total |
|---|---|---|---|---|---|---|
| Representation | 6 | 1 | 5 | — | 6 | 18 |
| Takeover | 13 | — | — | — | — | 13 |
| Agree with T.U. | — | 1 | 1 | 3 | 1 | 6 |
| Political | — | 1 | 2 | 1 | 1 | 5 |
| All Joined | — | 3 | 1 | — | — | 4 |
| Consultation | — | 3 | — | — | — | 3 |

important, and it is necessary to consider some of these responses in more detail.

A few make just a general reference to the takeover, sometimes adding a mention of the new management.

'I joined because of the takeover by —. Formerly there were good staff-management relationships, but the new people were high-handed.'

The rumour of redundancies also had a great effect. Some who had previously stayed out now decided to join when 'there was a threat of redundancies . . .'–a common statement. They joined because they saw the union as a means of protection but this was not the only reaction. Not the policies themselves, even redundancy, but the lack of communication provokes several respondents.

'I was brought up with a distaste of trade unions. At first I agreed with —'s redundancy policy as necessary, but there seemed no means of finding out about future policy.'

Another gives a similar response, but with more militancy.

'I had thought of it [i.e. joining]. It was brought to a head by the redundancies. You can get information from the power of a union.'

Those not brought into the union by either the takeover or the threat of redundancy directly, could still be encouraged indirectly by the A.Sc.W.'s show of strength over these issues. The following are two individuals with otherwise opposite views:

'I had been on the railways, and was keen on trade unions. But not at first at — because the A.Sc.W. was

160

weak. I joined because its strength showed over the take-over.'

'There was talk of redundancy. The A.Sc.W. had some success in doing something for those redundant. It's useful to belong to such a body. You need to belong to an organization in a large company. I had no former sympathy with trade unions.'

Some of these members may leave the union when conditions return to normal, but it would seem that the majority, having taken the step of joining and realizing the advantages, are likely to remain members.

Their reasons for joining are very much as one would expect. That is, in terms of the hypothesis put forward, their employment experience has made them aware of their divorce from management. It is perhaps interesting to compare these and the following responses with an American assessment of the causes of dissatisfaction among engineers which are thought to lead to unionization. The list is quite lengthy and gives no weight to the different factors. However, those mentioned include, under 'professional treatment'–'1. a feeling among engineers that they were not identified with management, 2. inadequate channels of communication between top management and non-supervisory engineers, 3. inadequate recognition of the engineer as a professional employee'; under 'personal treatment' –'1. inadequate recognition and treatment of the engineer as an individual, 2. lack of broad classifications and appropriate titles by which the engineer could measure his progress . . . 5. a feeling of insecurity of employment'; and under 'financial treatment'–'1. engineering salaries not commensurate with fundamental contribution, 2. too small a differential between the pay of engineers and members of the skilled trades'.[1] Even this selective list of the more significant items surely shows that it is not the particular factor which is important but the situation which allows that factor to exist. Many of them go together in clusters, because a certain type of work requires particular employer-employee relationships. These relationships are then reflected in the detailed factors mentioned.

The respondents themselves do not see their membership

[1] R. E. Walton, *The Impact of the Professional Engineering Union,* Harvard University, 1961, p. 21.

of a union as a result of any single factor. As has already been noted with the members of Branch A, their responses are a mixture of several feelings—non-identification with the new management, fear of unemployment, lack of communication. Of the other branch members, the largest number (18) are quite clear on why they joined the A.Sc.W.—they wanted representation on salaries and conditions of work. Usually this is put simply—'the need for representation', 'financial benefit', but some are more expansive.

> 'Complaints by manual workers' unions are always seen to; those by individuals are ignored. When the A.Sc.W. complained they got somewhere.'

Wright Mills was quoted in an earlier chapter on the relative influence of principled and practical acceptance of unionism. Some of the Branch A members who joined because of the takeover and some of the 18 just discussed can perhaps be described as accepting unionism on practical grounds despite a lack of principled support, but the proportion should not be exaggerated. They are perhaps best treated as an intermediate group between those who definitely accept unions on principle and those who are merely reluctant or casual members. In the former category are the 6 who state explicitly that they joined because they agreed with the principles of trade unionism, together with the 5 who joined for political reasons, that is, because of their left-wing views—'as a socialist I feel I should be in a trade union'. Seemingly more reluctant, though even here not absolutely so, are the 4 who think of the A.Sc.W. more as a body for consultation than for bargaining.

> 'There was a Works Committee for manual workers at the factory, but communications were very bad for the staff. The A.Sc.W. was a better medium for communication.'

The only obviously casual joiners are those who became members 'because everyone else [in their work group] did so'. One American study of a professional engineering union has shown that only about one-half of the members join 'with some conviction', the rest reluctantly or casually.[1] The present group are obviously difficult to classify in this way. Goldstein,

[1] Goldstein, op. cit., p. 216.

in his study, probably did not have in mind the same division as did Mills, since someone who joins for the practical benefits can hardly be described as reluctant or casual. Accepting this sort of division it is probable that some three-quarters of the respondents joined with conviction.

As Goldstein himself points out[1] an individual's reason for joining does not necessarily determine his future attitude towards the union, a reluctant joiner, for example, perhaps becoming an ardent advocate. This may be the case with some of the present respondents. They show a high degree of unanimity about the main function of the A.Sc.W.—37 of them see this as being the improvement of salaries and conditions. Here again, however, the findings fit fairly closely those of Goldstein, with perhaps a little less emphasis, that 'all through the interviews we find the theme of the Council as a defensive, protective organization, rather than an aggressive militant one'.[2] In those branches of the A.Sc.W. where some sort of grievance procedure existed, however, it did seem to have more than the symbolic function that it apparently had for his respondents.

There are only a few other ideas about the function of the A.Sc.W. A small minority again stress the idea of consultation (6).

'Talking over the problems of staff with management.'
'Presentation of general view to management on the feelings of technical people.'

Five others are more concerned about its wider function of helping to determine science policy.

'Organizing of people employed in science in order to have some say in policy with regard to the use of science.'

In an interesting American study of the attitudes of unorganized engineers towards collective bargaining, the author came to the conclusion that 'the number of critical statements in this and other chapters about salary levels and personal salary adjustments indicates that dissatisfaction on these grounds is a major potential cause of unionization among engineers and scientists'.[3] His evidence certainly supports this

[1] Ibid., p. 224.      [2] Ibid., p. 225.
[3] J. W. Riegel, *Collective Bargaining as Viewed by Unorganised Engineers and Scientists*, University of Michigan, 1959, p. 99.

conclusion. Only 10 per cent of his respondents were favourable towards collective bargaining, together with 8 per cent who favoured professional society action. Fifty per cent, it may be noted, were strongly against.[1] Comparing ten different companies, the 'score' in each on satisfaction with salary related perfectly with the 'score' on opposition to collective bargaining.[2] Of those who argued for unionization, the largest number (18 out of 44) did so in order 'to obtain higher salaries and more equitable salary adjustments', and 10 more because 'it would or could be advantageous'.[3]

In view of this there is some interest in considering the satisfactions of the present respondents with their salary, and with use made of knowledge and skill, prospects for promotion and status. The responses are divided into the satisfied, the dissatisfied, and the intermediate not wholly satisfied. The greatest degree of dissatisfaction certainly is with salary (12 dissatisfied, 9 not wholly satisfied, 28 satisfied), but the satisfied group is still more than twice the size of the other. The situation is very similar for the use made of knowledge and skill (9, 11, 29) and for prospects for promotion (7, 16, 26). Only with status is there a good deal more satisfaction (7, 8, 34). A common reason for satisfaction with this last is that, apart from its financial aspects, it was of little concern to the individual, and the financial aspects were in any case referred to explicitly. This is in contrast to the respondents in the Institution of Metallurgists or the Engineers' Guild. Comparing these with the A.Sc.W. members, it does seem that the latter are on the whole less satisfied. There would seem to be a connection between dissatisfaction, particularly with salary, and union membership, but even among unionists the dissatisfied form a minority. Nor is dissatisfaction with salary by any means of sole importance.

Almost as interesting as the members' own reasons for joining are their opinions on why others do not do so. Most respondents give several opinions, but the two most frequent responses present a good idea of the two differing attitudes. Twenty-four believe that the others are too superior or snobbish.

[1] Ibid., p. 3. As the author points out, however, 'there is no implication in this report . . . that the substantial majority of professionals in our sample who oppose collective bargaining is likely to be an enduring one' (p. 11).

[2] Ibid., p. 103.   [3] Ibid., p. 13.

TRADE UNIONISTS

'They think themselves above the manual workers—respectable.
'They think it's beneath them.'
'Professional snobbishness.'
'Not the "done thing".'
'Trade unions are *infra dig.*'

In contrast to this group, who no doubt see themselves as making a realistic acceptance of trade unions, are those who are a little less certain. Twenty-two responses suggest the belief that on the whole scientists and engineers can look after themselves.

'It can do nothing for them. Qualifications give them choice of jobs.'
'They think it's no use to them—they're probably right.'

The other responses, which are anyway much less frequent, are not easy to classify in this way. Eight think that others have political objections to the union.

'It's too much allied to the T.U.C.—left wing.'
'Inbred distrust of trade unions—left. Many identify with the middle class, having come from the working class. They think it communist.'
'Misguided idea that unions are pro-Labour.'

Another 6 are rather similar to the second group above, and stress the individuality of engineers and scientists.

'Qualified people are thinking people. They think for themselves, are independent. They don't need to join, they can easily move.'
'They do better on their own.'

A further 4 believe that non-joiners have principled objections, and 4 that engineers and scientists are too pro-management, either through principle or because they think that union membership would prejudice their chances of promotion. Only 3 responses mention ignorance of trade unions.

In view of the lack of activity in at least three of the branches, it is perhaps rather surprising that the great majority of respondents are satisfied with the A.Sc.W. and what it does for them. Thirty-two have no suggestions for further activities in which they would like to see the union engage.

'No. It's doing a good job, especially over redundancy. This is a good branch.'

'They should carry on the way they are now.'

'No. It shouldn't be too big or militant.'

Of the suggestions that are made the main ones are for more local meetings (5)—especially asked for by members of the general branch, more interest in members (4), more activities concerned with science policy (3), and more active negotiation (3). Somewhat similar responses are found when, given the respondents' satisfaction or dissatisfaction with the four aspects of their work, one considers what more, if anything, they think the A.Sc.W. should do about any of them. This prompting draws out a few more suggestions, but there are still 21 respondents who feel that the union does quite enough about all these matters. Many of them take the realistic view that it does as much as it can considering its weakness and the attitudes of its members.

'It tries, but there are not sufficient members.'

'It isn't the A.Sc.W.'s fault if not enough is done. The members don't give it their full support.'

Ten respondents would like the A.Sc.W. to concern itself more with the use made of the technologist's knowledge and skill, and 8 want more concern with salaries. Again it would seem that dissatisfaction with salary is not of overriding importance in unionization. These members are at least as much concerned with the work that they are doing. Here are some typical responses.

'The A.Sc.W. should press for better use of skill.'

'By ensuring the use of highly qualified men in jobs that demand it.'

'It should make suggestions to management, but that's difficult. More moving around would be useful, but perhaps not profitable' (i.e. to management). This same respondent comments: 'Courses useful to management are not necessarily the most useful to the individual, because he is more restricted.'

'It should try to get management to foster more training, to keep men up to date in advances.'

'It should get a minimum wage for qualifications, do more to get levelling-off. There should be equal treatment, or at least a minimum, for qualifications' (i.e. in different subjects).

'It should make suggestions to management. Salaries should be according to qualification and responsibility.'

Most of the respondents are probably thinking of normal collective bargaining, but as can be seen, there is an important moderate, 'make suggestions to management' strain.

Three-quarters of the respondents have a favourable attitude towards collective bargaining as a means of dealing with the problems of scientists and engineers, 3 of the remainder are unfavourable towards it, and 8 are doubtful. The great majority of the favourable (18 out of 38) believe that there is no other way of dealing with their problems. Some of them make the point that as far as they are concerned they are just like any other group of employees.

'Scientists are no different from others. There's too much individualism—scientists are really interdependent.'

'I don't see the arguments about being a professional. The brilliant ones can still get ahead.'

'In private industry there are employers' organizations. A professional man should have an organization to put forward his views and problems. Individual bargaining suits the employer.'

Very close to these are the 8 who think that individuals have great difficulty in negotiating for themselves, especially, according to some, because of the engineer's mainly technical training.

'It is the only fair method which ensures that the more reticent colleagues who may not feel capable of negotiating on their own behalf are not forgotten by management.'

A few respondents qualify their answers to some extent by saying that collective bargaining is necessary in the large firm, but not perhaps elsewhere.

'It isn't possible to negotiate as an individual in a large concern.'

'There's no other method in a big firm, where people are lumped together. Perhaps not if things were more personal.'

A few more see it as being suitable for the lower grades of technologists and technicians, but not really for senior men.

It is difficult to explain why there should be even 3 union members who have an unfavourable attitude towards collective bargaining. One is obviously a reluctant joiner, with a clear professional attitude.

'I joined because the Institution of Electrical Engineers does not protect its members like the B.M.A.'

Another seems to accept the union only while it remains weak. His opposition to collective bargaining is that 'a man should be judged on his merits'.

Of the doubtful group, some feel that it is undesirable but necessary, others fear that it might lead to loss of individuality or jeopardize their good relations with management.

'I think it's rather "collective representation". There's a need to keep up with the general rise in wages, etc., but I don't like the idea of forcing as much as possible out of an employer.'

'It's not the ideal way. There should not be the necessity for it. People should be paid on their individual merits, but at present there's no alternative.'

'No, for salary—that's personal for professionals. Yes, for conditions of service.'

'No, it isn't suitable, but it's the only way. I wouldn't always follow the union if I disagreed with it.'

Five of the doubtful group and two of those who are unfavourable are in fact members of Branch A, where the take-over crisis probably forced them to join.

The question of professional unions and politics has already been touched on in a general way, so it is useful to compare the earlier observations with the opinions of these members. The conclusion that such unions are not identified with left-wing politics is borne out here. Twenty-four of the respondents believe that trade unionism need have no connection at all with politics.

'Trade unions should not have anything to do with politics.'

'Government elections are for politics.'

'Trade unionism is merely concerned with conditions of employment.'

Another 5 think that unionism does necessarily involve some political aspects, but they are doubtful about the morality of this, preferring the unions to keep out of politics wherever possible.

The remaining 20 members all believe that trade unionism and politics are necessarily connected, but they are equally divided between those who see the connection in party terms and those who do not. The latter take the view that the union's concern with its members' interests must inevitably require it to concern itself also with national economic policy and any other matters which would affect employment.

'Bound to be, especially in a big union, because the Government determines economic policy. Not a party matter.'

'Inevitable, but not necessarily socialist. The Government must consult the unions.'

'Not necessarily connected with the Labour Party. They should make representations to Governments. Some things can only be done by the Government.'

This group think that there is a connection with politics in general, but not with any particular party. The other is more definite, that trade unionism has to have a political wing—the Labour Party.

'The working class needs a political wing to further its ends.'

'They should be left wing, because the employers are against the working man.'

This chapter has attempted to provide answers to two main questions: why a certain group of professional people, scientists and engineers, join a union, and what sort of a union they make of it. The answers to a large extent fit into the hypotheses put forward. Joining a union is a sign of a class attitude, one which the hypothesis predicts as more likely for those who do not share in the exercise of authority as part of management, and even more likely for those whose work emphasizes their separation. The trade-union members considered are almost all in the first situation. More important, union organization is strongest among the latter. This is the main reason why there is a high degree of unionization in the electrical engineering industry. The members see their own reasons for joining as being mostly a desire for a body to improve their salaries and conditions, to put forward their views to management, or to serve as a vehicle of communication. One would expect such responses from those who realize their separation from management. For most of them membership of a union does not seem to be the result of dissatisfaction with their salary alone.

The major fact about the A.Sc.W. is its weakness, especially amongst qualified workers. This is the main indication of the influence of status attitudes amongst engineers and scientists. The results of this weakness were seen in several of the local branches, where only a minimum of union activity takes place. In those branches where it is stronger, it is undoubtedly able to do a good deal more. Even here, however, there is still a widespread feeling of moderation amongst the members. Representation, rather than negotiation, is often stressed, and militant action, especially striking, is opposed. Class attitudes are also clearly stronger in some members than in others. There are those whose class consciousness extends beyond the situation of their particular group and beyond the work relationships in their particular company, giving them a greater feeling of identification with other groups of workers, and leading to a belief in the Labour Party as the political wing of the labour movement. The majority, however, have a much more restricted consciousness of class. Their class attitudes show in their membership of a trade union, but whilst accepting collective bargaining they still wish to preserve a special relationship with management. Moreover, their consciousness is restricted only to their particular group, without extending to include other groups or to relationships out of work. The influence of status ideas is still strong, even within a class organization. This fact is still explicable in terms of the employment situation. These are, it must be remembered, a comparatively well-paid, proportionately small group of employees, performing work which for the most part is interesting and congenial.

# Part IV

# CONCLUSION

# CHAPTER NINE

# Professional Employees

Scientists and engineers are, as we have argued throughout, a vitally important occupational group in industrial society. They are, comparatively, few in number, but they have grown and will no doubt continue to grow rapidly. So, too, will the industries and processes that technologists have created, and which, in turn, create a greater demand for their services.

In the political sphere technologists, despite the great importance of their expertise, do not seem to have secured for themselves, or even tried to secure, any great degree of power or influence. No modern society could properly be described as a 'technocracy' in the political sense, nor could one argue that technologists are the controllers of industry, although there is little doubt that many of them, particularly engineers, are increasingly to be found in management, even top management positions.

One aim of this study has been to explore a part of Merton's 'entire range of allegiances', because these allegiances are believed to be important in determining the distribution of power both within industry and in the wider society. In particular, we have concentrated upon the relationship of technologists to those with authority in industry, especially where it is dependent on the technical organization of production, and the ideas about the system of social stratification that derive from this relationship. In this way the study has tried to pursue its other main aim of testing a theory of social stratification and of the ideologies related to it.

This theory holds that there are two forms of stratification in modern British society, class and status, and that the two are closely related. Stratification by class, the division between those with power, especially economic power, and those without, is considered basic. Status, which is based on the differential distribution of honour and prestige, arises out of the pre-existing class situation. It derives from the attempt of those with power to legitimize their position. They claim that this power is a result of their possession of some criterion of superiority. Their ideology emphasizes the gradation of society into a hierarchy according to the possession of the honorific criteria, and with themselves at or near the apex.

It is most important to realize that these two forms of stratification are analytically distinct, if only because in practice they are inextricably confused. To the sociologist both are objective systems, in that they have an external reality to the individual. Given this, the major interest must be in their subjective influences, and even more, their effect on behaviour. Ideas and attitudes, and the actions which result from them, can be classified as tending towards either a class or status type, rather than as being purely one or the other. That is, there is a steady continuum from a status ideology to a class ideology.

The ideal type of status consciousness, at one extreme, involves a complete acceptance of the ideology of the ruling group, and the individual's view of stratification would be that society was arranged in a hierarchy, with those possessing the greatest degree of honour and prestige at the top. The legitimate authority of the latter would be respected. At the other extreme the ideal type of class consciousness would be a rejection of the claims of those with power, and the belief that this power must be challenged. The difference between the two is that one is an acceptance, the other a rejection of the ideology offered by the ruling group to justify its position, and there can obviously be a whole range of degrees of acceptance or rejection, from wholehearted at one end, through the various 'mixed' stages to wholehearted at the other.

The major factor in determining whether or not this ideology will be accepted is believed to be the employment situation of the group. Basically this can be reduced to two elements. First, whether the individual is one who shares in the exercise of authority. Rejection of the ideology can only be expected from those who do not, but it is likely that others who expect later to share in this exercise, through promotion, will also to a large extent accept the ideology. Secondly, given the position of subordination, rejection is most likely from individuals whose employment experience emphasizes the fact. The important factors here are not merely market situation—low income and lack of opportunity, but also work situation—such things as strict supervision, lesser personal control over work, organization in large, impersonal work groups, and so forth.

In the case of scientists and engineers, at least, there are two forms of collective organization which are associated with the two ideologies, professional associations and trade unions. Professionalism is traditionally connected with independent, fee-paid practitioners, but recently a number of occupational groups, consisting largely of employees, have claimed to be, and have been accepted as professionals. These have organized themselves largely on the lines of the traditional models, and have formed professional associations. However, the bodies they have created are believed to be in many ways different from those of the traditional professionals. It is therefore necessary to consider the actual functions that they perform, to see how they are different. It is also necessary to show that these functions are closely related to a status ideology. Since they are bodies which represent employees, it is necessary, finally, to see whether there are any tendencies towards class attitudes or activities.

The connection between trade unionism and class is more obvious. Trade unions are a collective expression of conflict of interest, and collective bargaining is an institutionalized form of this conflict. A study of trade unions would therefore need to show that they are strongest amongst those groups who have already been described as being more likely to reject a status ideology in favour of a class type. However, since this rejection is not necessarily complete, the study would also need to show whether some status attitudes still remained, and how important they were.

A general survey of the employment of scientists and engineers provides a limited amount of background material. Just under a half are employed in private industry, a seventh in the nationalized industries, a tenth in central government, a fifth in local government, while nearly a quarter are engaged in education. As was seen, however, there are wide differences in the employment of various particular specialists. The five major private employing industries are electrical engineering, chemicals, plant and machinery, aircraft and building and contracting. Little is known about the type of work done, beyond the fact that in these major industries the highest proportions engaged in research and development are around 50 per cent. Most of the remainder are probably in administrative positions, though in electrical engineering in particular, some are engaged in work very close to production. As an indication of typical salaries, medians, for the 40–45 age-group, ranged from £1,485 p.a. for civil engineers to £2,000 p.a. for physicists in 1959–60.

Even this limited amount of information, however, can provide a starting-point. It is clear that a high proportion of scientists and engineers are in management positions–they share in the exercise of authority. This means that a substantially greater number can, and do, reasonably expect to move into such positions. Those who are not part of management will often be performing relatively independent and interesting research and development work. On the whole they are a fairly well-paid group. In terms of our theory, then, one would expect status attitudes to predominate, so that it is the status type of collective organization, professionalism, which is dealt with first.

In the study of the actual functions of the professional associations, one fact emerged quite clearly, that the major concern of most of these bodies is with technical, study and educational activities: that is, with furthering the particular technology, not with furthering the interests of particular technologists. To this extent these bodies are not concerned with status–they are like other learned societies, but equally, to the same extent, they are not concerned with professional matters as they are understood here. The traditional professional associations of course concern themselves with their special branch of learning, but not to the same overwhelming extent as do many of these bodies.

However, they also have other functions which are more obviously professional. The function of qualification is the most important of these, a fact which shows the status nature of these associations most clearly. It is shown both in the form of organization and in its limits. The occupational group combine to mark themselves off as a grade in the hierarchy, technical knowledge being an honorific criterion, but the use made of the qualification is left entirely to the individual, who retains his personal relationship with his employer. This purpose of membership has not always existed. The early engineering institutions limited their membership to the knowledgeable in order to preserve the high technical tone of their proceedings; only later did this get reversed so that membership, and the letters after the name, itself became a qualification.

This situation is significantly different from that of the independent professionals. They, too, are concerned with status, and they limit their membership to those accepted as qualified. They go further than this, however, and obtain a monopoly of the occupation. The professional body secures this by providing a hallmark of competence, and thus guaranteeing that its members ought to be able to perform certain tasks satisfactorily. The professional qualification becomes, in effect, a licence to practise. Scientists and engineers have not obtained, and probably could not obtain such a monopoly position. They are employed in a wide variety of jobs, and sometimes there may be no easy way of distinguishing them from technicians or even skilled craftsmen. As employees, the determination of the type of work that they do is in the hands not of themselves, nor of the professional association, but of the employer. He decides whom he wishes to employ in any particular position. The relationship between employer and employee is very different from that between practitioner and client. Professional monopoly is designed to protect the client from the incompetent, but an employer does not need this protection. He is the judge of the individual's work, and he has the power of dismissal.

The qualification bestowed by the professional association is, then, much more like a university degree than a licence to practise. It is merely a status attribute. How little more the professional associations can achieve is shown when one considers the two other main functions of the traditional professional body. The professional conduct function, the maintenance of the ethical code which is often thought to be so important, hardly exists for these bodies. Where it does, it applies only to the small minority of independent practitioners, or is so vague as to be of no practical use. Here again the reason is that these are employees. Independent professionals operate an ethical code to protect their long-term interests, but the relationship between employer and employee has no need of such a code. The engineer or scientist has the same basic reason for working well as any other employee—if he does not he may be dismissed. He may have much more loyalty to management, but this is an indication of his status ideology, not of his professionalism.

The other major function is that of professional protection. The traditional professions do not merely grant qualifications, they control the use made of them. They are able to obtain a monopoly and to further their financial and other interests because they are independent. When the professionals are employees, however, it becomes much more difficult to perform this function. The old professions can act according to a status ideology and thereby collectively further their interest. Employed professionals are much less able to do this. Their associations of course feel the need to do so—'to maintain the status of . . .' as they usually put it—but when they try they are caught in a paradox. Their members are employees, and their incomes are paid by their employers. Therefore the only effective method would be to negotiate or bargain with employers. This, however, would be an expression of conflict of interest, which is an idea repugnant to their status attitudes. In the event very little is done. Most of the efforts in this respect are designed to strengthen the hand of individuals, and to provide information for employers, rather than to take collective action. In a few cases amongst the bodies studied there were definite signs of a certain amount of collective bargaining, showing that class pressures are of some importance even within the professional associations.

The study of the activities of these associations supports the arguments, firstly, that these bodies are expressions of a status ideology; secondly, that because their members are employees, they differ in certain important ways from the traditional associations of independent professionals; and thirdly, that because of the nature of the employment of some of their members, there are some tendencies towards activities of a class type.

Further support is gained from studying the members of these bodies. The first, the Institution of Metallurgists, is something of an exception in having very few study activities, but this fact does make it more clearly a professional body than many of the others dealt with in this work. Nevertheless, although it has few study activities, the service most used by the members is that of the technical publications, and the further services most demanded are those which are part of the study function. These facts by themselves demonstrate the great importance of this function for these bodies.

The members themselves are well aware of the central place of the qualifying function. The need to get a qualification is given by the majority as their reason for joining, and no other single response is given by more than a few members. Nearly one-half of them also believe the Institution's main function to be the conduct of examinations. There is thus little doubt that the members largely see the association in status terms, which is, in fact, the way they want it to be.

However, some of the members do mention professional protection, a quarter, for example, thinking that the main function of the Institution is to raise the metallurgist's status, and to deal with salaries and conditions. This aspect was probed more closely later, by trying to discover the members' satisfaction with certain areas of their work experience. Overall satisfaction is obviously fairly high. The great majority are satisfied with the use made of their knowledge and skill, rather fewer with their status, and just under two-thirds with their prospects for promotion and their salary. In each case those doing technical work, that is those most likely to be in subordinate positions, are less satisfied than those in administration, those most likely to be part of management.

It would seem, however, that a number of those who are satisfied as well as those who are not, would like the Institution to do more about these things. Just over a half want more done about the use made of knowledge and skill and status, just under a half would like more concern with salaries and promotion. It is interesting that so many should want more done about the use made of knowledge and skill when they are mostly satisfied, and that a higher proportion should want the Institution to do more about status than want it to do more about salary, even though there was less satisfaction with the latter. This shows, firstly, that these members again see the Institution largely in status terms, and secondly, that they too are caught in the paradox already described. They would like to enjoy higher financial rewards, but they cannot bring themselves to pursue them directly by collective action. Instead they want the Institution to try to raise their status, hoping that greater financial rewards would follow from this.

These status attitudes are shown clearly in the methods suggested by which the Institution could do more. The most popular is 'more publicity'—the idea being that public opinion should be made more aware of their value, and so hold them in higher regard (and then, probably, pay them more). Another frequent response is for more educational work—this being designed to improve the use made of metallurgists and so also their status. Rather fewer want more 'general' education, that is to provide metallurgists with the non-technical skills which would make them more suitable for promotion to management positions.

A few show some inclination towards attitudes of a class type. Some mildly suggest consultation with management, others want the Institution to 'deal with salaries' (which could probably only be done by negotiation of some sort), and others again that it should set minimum salary levels (and, presumably, use the collective power of the occupational group to enforce them).

This conflict between status and class attitudes was studied more closely in the Engineers' Guild. Here is a body which has no function other than that of protection and which claims to be 'professional'. It opposes collective bargaining for qualified engineers as unprofessional and thus provides a good test for the hypothesis. According to this, if the Guild is to justify its existence at all it would have to tend towards collective bargaining. One would expect to find fairly influential class attitudes amongst its members.

A preliminary vindication of the hypothesis seems to result from the fact that only a small minority of those eligible are members of the Guild. Of those who are members very few have made any use of the services it provides, and most of them accept the weakness of the Guild. They argue that nothing could be done without more members, but this of course still fails to explain what the Guild would actually do even with a 100 per cent membership. It would then be only in the same position as those associations, like the Institution of Metallurgists, which already have a high membership.

There is little doubt that the members show a marked tendency towards class attitudes when compared with the metallurgists. The majority, of course, joined for the sort of reasons which are associated with a status ideology ('a desire to improve the status of engineers', a belief that the Guild was 'a good idea'), but a substantial number joined because they wanted a body to deal with salaries and conditions or 'a bargaining body'. Most of the latter are employed in industries where collective bargaining is already established. They seem to have joined not in order to escape the evils of trade unionism but to find a more appropriate body.

The same sort of division is found over the members' views on the main function of the Guild. The majority see its task as one of raising the status of engineers, but again a substantial minority think more in terms of a body to deal with salaries and conditions.

As with the metallurgists most of these engineers are satisfied with the four aspects of their work which were considered. Not unexpectedly, since this is a protective body, a higher proportion of these want the Guild to do more about them, though some seem to be quite satisfied. Again there is a division between those who think more in status terms, placing their faith in more publicity, and the smaller number who want collective bargaining. Between the two are those who suggest making representations to management, without actually bargaining.

When they are asked directly, the members are by no means hostile to the idea of collective bargaining. There is only a small majority against it, a few are doubtful, and most of those who think it suitable have reservations, but on the other hand the major objections are practical ones rather than principled.

The hypothesis would here seem to have been substantially correct. The Guild at present does very little, and it is weak. Since it now offers so little, it seems impossible for it to increase its membership by very much. Its only effective means of justifying itself would be to undertake collective bargaining, but unless conditions change it is not likely to do this, nor would it be acceptable anyway to the great majority of non-members. There are of course pressures in this direction. Status attitudes predominate amongst its members, but there are many whose ideas are more of a class type.

This study of the professional associations and some professional people has demonstrated the three points which were put forward earlier. Firstly, there has been shown to exist a connection between professionalism and a status ideology. Secondly, the fact that these are employed professionals has been shown to make this form of professionalism different from the traditional type. Thirdly, it has been shown that class attitudes, though not very strong, do exist, especially, as the hypothesis requires, amongst those employed in technical work. The professional associations are most unlikely to be affected by these pressures. Their predominant concern is with the study, educational and qualifying functions. Should there be any greater need and demand for protection it is to trade unionism that these employees will have to turn.

As yet, at least in private employment, the need does not appear to be very great. Most of this group still retains a status ideology, because of their favourable employment conditions. Nevertheless, class attitudes are to be found, and trade unions do exist. They are well established for this group in central and local government, in education, and in the nationalized industries. In most of them scientists and engineers form only a small part of the whole. Nearly a half of the total are employed in these four areas, and something like 70 to 80 per cent are probably members of a trade union. In private industry the position is entirely different. Only two bodies are of any importance: the British Association of Chemists, which with its membership of 2,000 (half of them fully qualified) has a coverage of about 5 per cent in the chemical industry, and the Association of Scientific Workers, which has 17,000 members, only a minority of whom are fully qualified, and has a lower coverage throughout the range of private industry.

Two reasons were advanced to explain this difference between public and private employment. The first is the difference in employment experience. In the former are found many of the familiar elements of bureaucratization—centralization, rational grading and promotion schemes, and greater impersonality. The total effect is to emphasize the office, the grade and the work group rather than the individual. It is to be contrasted with the administrative particularism which is common in private employment. The second reason is more important. The class situations, the division of authority, in private and public employment are not strictly comparable. There may be a division of authority, but there is not the same conflict of interest. Without this conflict, there is not the same need of the employer to legitimize his power by means of the status ideology. Trade unionism is therefore much more acceptable to both 'sides', especially in view of its instrumental value in a bureaucratic structure.

The trade unions which exist were seen to differ in many ways from those of manual workers. None of them is actually called a union, and many of them, even very large ones, are not registered under the Trade Union Acts. Only a very few are affiliated to the T.U.C. Their objections to the latter body are mainly political, but they are in any case unwilling to ally themselves with other parts of the labour movement. They lay a good deal of stress on democracy within the union, mostly in order to maintain a responsible leadership, and, as part of the same ideology, on co-operation with management. Although they are accepted for their instrumental value rather than for reasons of principle, they are seen less as bargaining bodies than as representative ones, placing great faith in rational persuasion. The extreme unwillingness to take strike action is a natural corollary of these attitudes.

The survey of trade unions made it clear that even though, as bargaining bodies, they are manifestations of class attitudes, their activities are still very much influenced by those of status. The more particular study of the A.Sc.W. shows this, as well as providing further information on the conditions under which trade unionism is most likely to be successful.

The analysis of the new recruits to the North-West Region demonstrated one important fact about the industries in which unionism for this group is mostly found. The great majority of these recruits were employed in the two major industries of electrical engineering and chemicals. This means that two other large employing industries, plant and machinery and aircraft, are very much under-represented, but little could be said about the reasons for this. However, the two former industries were not equally represented, as there were proportionately many more recruits from the electrical engineering industry, and the reasons for this are significant. Although the great majority from both were employed in technical work, that is, they were not part of management, in electrical engineering many more were in work which would emphasize the fact. Their jobs were often close to those of actual production, such as testing, drawing up specifications, designing, or even production itself. This type of work is likely to involve organization in larger work groups, lesser control over the job, more supervision, and more routinization—in all, those conditions which will emphasize their subordinate positions.

The relatively greater success of the union in the electrical engineering industry is also evident when the Merseyside branches are considered. Of the five, the two in this industry are undoubtedly the strongest, best organized and most active. The other three branches, the largest of which is for employees in the chemical industry, are much less active and more loosely organized. They can hardly be said to engage at all in collective bargaining at the local level.

The study of the members of these branches again shows the importance in unionization of those situations which emphasize subordination. The most dramatic example is the case of the branch in a company which had recently experienced a take-over. This event had a catalytic effect, by highlighting the position of these employees. They now felt insecure, part of a larger organization, subject to new and unknown policies from a new, unknown management. Probably some of these feelings will diminish, and some members will resign, but once well established such a branch is likely to remain, if only because it has cleared the major hurdle of demonstrating its value. This firm, in fact, has few qualified men in work close to production, but the other electrical engineering branch was formed in a plant where nearly everyone is in production work.

In the branch affected, the takeover provides by far the most important reason for joining the union. Other members joined mostly because they wanted representation on salaries and conditions. These, and the fairly high proportion who joined on grounds of principle, because of agreement with the principles of trade unionism, or for political reasons, were clearly mainly influenced by class attitudes. Only a few seem to have been reluctant or casual joiners. The great majority believe that the main function of the union is to improve their conditions.

Most of them also see collective bargaining as a suitable way of dealing with the problems of qualified engineers and scientists, the majority thinking that there is really no other way. Again, however, there is a minority who think collective bargaining unsuitable, or who are doubtful about it.

As far as their own work experience is concerned, then, most of the members accept trade unionism. They are obviously strongly influenced by class attitudes, even though a small minority still seem to think rather more in status terms. When class in its wider, total society sense is considered, these latter attitudes are clearly much more influential. Almost one-half of the respondents think that there should be no connection between trade unionism and politics, and a half of those who believe that there should be, saw the connection just as one with politics in general, with unions as another pressure group. This leaves only about one-fifth who saw the connection as an essential one between the industrial and political wings of the same labour movement.

Trade unionism, then, amongst scientists and engineers, apart from those in public employment, is weak. This is, from all that has been said, what one would expect. Again, even where it exists it is still influenced by the status attitudes of many of its members. Nevertheless, it does exist, and in those areas where the theory would require it: in those industries where engineers and scientists are employed on a large scale on work which is divorced from and clearly subordinate to management. The future of these unions depends on the future employment of the group that they serve. Undoubtedly, more technologists will be employed throughout industry. They will probably be used increasingly in management positions, but at the same time changing technology will also require many more of them to work in production processes. The most likely result of this will be that those with the highest qualifications will occupy the former positions, leaving the others for the lesser qualified.

The argument of this study may be briefly summarized. Many scientists and engineers are employed in positions in which they either share directly in the exercise of authority, or in which their work gives them the feeling of being close to management. They therefore accept the employers' ideology of stratification, that they are part of a graded hierarchy. This has its concrete expression in the professional associations. Of those who do not share in the exercise of authority, some will experience work conditions which emphasize the fact of their subordination. These individuals are likely to have attitudes which are more of a class type, and elements of this are found within the professional associations. The more these work conditions are present, the stronger will be the class attitudes, until eventually there comes a major change. For the individual this means a recognition of a conflict of interest with the employer, an acceptance of collective bargaining and membership of a trade union. This step is crucial as far as behaviour is concerned, but it does not involve a complete change of ideology. The class viewpoint is largely restricted to the employment situation and does not extend to cover other groups. Status attitudes remain, and have a strong effect on the activities of the union.

The intention in this work has been to throw light on several matters. It has provided a certain amount of information on a particularly important occupational group in modern society. As a result of the theoretical approach which has been used, it has brought into question the meaning of professionalism when applied to employees. Finally, it has provided some vindication of the theoretical approach. This case study has shown the value of considering social stratification in terms of both class and status, each having its effect on individuals' attitudes and behaviour, and of seeking out the factors which predispose towards one or the other. It has also provided evidence of the way in which the two sets of attitudes and types of behaviour are linked, by emphasizing the function of a status ideology in securing legitimization of the power of particular groups.

Many problems of course remain. The major need is for further study of the factors which give rise to trade unionism. This should try to provide not only more knowledge about the technologists dealt with here, but should extend to the lower grades of technicians, a rapidly expanding group of workers who should provide a good test of our hypothesis. The most fruitful way of doing this would be by making a study of whole firms. It would then be possible to take into account all the technicians and technologists employed, to obtain very much clearer data than has been possible in this study on the type of work that they do, to consider all the bodies that they belong to and their attitudes, in the way that has been done here.

Of course other groups of white-collar workers also deserve attention, even manual workers could fruitfully be studied in a search for the influences of status ideology. Such research into class attitudes within industry, however, is comparatively easy. In the absence of studies which would justify it, it would be dangerous to generalize from information about relationships

at the workplace to relationships outside. The authority structure at work is relatively straightforward and clear-cut, outside
it may be much less so. How far the position at work of scientists
and engineers, or indeed of any other group, determines their
place and behaviour in the wider society remains a matter for
debate and further study.

# APPENDIX

# Methods Used in the Study

The first stages of the study involved the collection of the literary material used in Chapters 4 and 7. This was obtained from all the professional associations and trade unions which appeared likely to be relevant. It was followed by a number of interviews with central and local officials. As this material was analysed the various bodies were considered for more detailed study. It was important, not that the bodies should be typical, since this was not to be a study of all engineers and scientists, but that they should be appropriate for the theoretical structure of the work. The bodies are not, however, in any way peculiar. They are all three well known and respected in their different fields.

The Institution of Metallurgists was thought suitable because it is a professional body which has most of its members in private industry, and because it tries to exercise the protective function. The Association of Scientific Workers was chosen because it is the most important union in private industry. The Engineers' Guild is unique, and it is fortunate that it exists, since it serves very well as an intermediate between the other two bodies.

For the three bodies dealt with in detail two methods of inquiry have been used – the postal questionnaire and personal interviewing.

## 1. Institution of Metallurgists

With the Institution of Metallurgists it seemed desirable to try to get a wide coverage of members on a limited number of questions. It was in any case likely that the members of this body in the Merseyside area would be unrepresentative, both in terms of numbers and of the type of work performed. A postal questionnaire therefore seemed the most desirable method.

This was sent to a 10 per cent sample of the whole membership in the period September–November 1961. The sample was stratified by grade, and for each grade names were arranged alphabetically and, starting from a random point in the first ten, every tenth name was selected. This gave 56 Students, 102 Licentiates, 202 Associates, and 81 Fellows, 441 in all.

The questionnaires were then sent out, together with an explanatory letter and a stamped return envelope. After two weeks a first reminder was sent, and two weeks after this a second, together with another copy of the questionnaire and stamped return envelope. Table 1 shows the individual and cumulative gross response rates.

TABLE 1

*Response Rate (per cent)*

| | Individual | | | Cumulative | | |
|---|---|---|---|---|---|---|
| | *1* | *2* | *3* | *1* | *2* | *3* |
| Student | 56 | 63 | 75 | 56 | 83 | 96·5 |
| Licentiate | 44 | 33·5 | 37 | 44 | 62 | 76 |
| Associate | 40·5 | 35 | 35 | 40·5 | 61·5 | 74·5 |
| Fellow | 45 | 44·5 | 36 | 45 | 70 | 81·5 |
| Total | 44 | 39 | 38 | 44 | 65 | 79 |

These are gross rates which include all replies received. Of the total of 347, 61 could not be used, the respondent having refused to co-operate, retired, gone abroad, or taken up other work totally unconnected with metallurgy. This left 65 per cent usable questionnaires overall: 71 per cent for Students, 72 per cent for Licentiates, 63·4 per cent for Associates, and 56·25 per cent for Fellows. The large proportion of retired members explains the figure in the last grade. The differences in response rates between grades is not very great, but they are in any case usually treated separately in the discussion.

The total response rate, for a postal survey, is quite high. This is probably due to the fairly advanced educational level of these respondents, but other contributory factors may have been the shortness of the questionnaire, and the possible interest of the inquiry to the members.[1] The need to have a fairly short questionnaire does seem to make the postal survey unsuitable for more complex inquiries.

The major problem, of course, is to identify the non-respondents, and to determine how far those who reply are representative of the whole. One suggested method of meeting this problem is to take successive samples of non-respondents, with the final sample being contacted personally.[2] In this instance the last step would have been prohibitively expensive, and anyway the complexity of the procedure seemed to outweigh the advantages.

The only feasible method of providing a check of some sort is to compare the three sets of responses, treating the second and third sets as 100 per cent samples of non-respondents. Assume then that a particular group is less willing to respond for some reason. If the degree of unwillingness is constant no matter how many times they are contacted, then this group will form a proportionately greater part of each successive set of non-respondents, and this should be reflected in a smaller total response. The Table above shows that this can have happened only to a small extent, if at all, and not equally for each grade. (A falling response rate would anyway be expected if one assumes, reasonably, a trait of 'inertia in replying to letters' unassociated with other factors.)

On the other hand the unwillingness to respond may not be constant. It may be overcome by a greater stimulus, in the form of bothersome reminder letters. In this case the particular group would form a greater proportion of each set of respondents. In fact there is no evidence that this has happened. With some factors, qualification for example, the pattern in each set of responses is substantially the same. With others, for example the answers on satisfaction with the four aspects of work, any difference between the first and second sets of responses always seems to be reversed between the second and third. This may be significant, but in what way it is impossible to tell. It appears to be purely random.

[1] For a very full discussion of postal surveys see C. Scott, 'Research on Mail Surveys', *Journal of the Royal Statistical Society*, Series A (General), vol. 124, 1961, pp. 143–205.
[2] M. A. Al-Badry, 'A Sampling Procedure for Mailed Questionnaires', *Journal of the American Statistical Society*, vol. 51, 1956, pp. 209–27.

It cannot be said from these considerations that there is no bias in the returns. They point to the conclusion, however, that any bias there may be is unlikely to be very marked.

## 2. *Engineers' Guild and A.Sc.W.*

For the study of the Engineers' Guild and the Association of Scientific Workers it was considered most desirable to carry out personal interviews of members in one area rather than to conduct a postal survey of a sample of the membership.

In the case of the Guild the names of the members living within the area covered by the Liverpool telephone directory (which extends to just short of Southport in the north and Chester in the south, and includes St. Helens, Warrington, the Runcorn-Widnes area and the Wirral) were obtained from the North-West area secretary. The interviews were carried out in the periods May–June and September 1961. Respondents with a telephone were sent an introductory letter and were then telephoned to make the appointment for the interview. The remainder were given a date and time in the introductory letter when the interviewer would call. The wording suggested that this visit would be either to carry out the interview or to arrange another appointment. In fact the former was really intended, and almost all respondents took it in this way. They were asked to reply only if the appointment was not convenient. This procedure was designed to make refusal difficult, but none of the respondents, if they saw it in this way, appeared to resent it. Quite a high proportion, especially of those with telephones, were able to have the interview at their office, the rest were seen in their homes. Of the 46 members contacted only two were unwilling to be interviewed.

The procedure was much the same with the A.Sc.W. members. In this case the basis of selection was membership of a Merseyside branch (including Southport), and the names were obtained through branch secretaries. These were also useful in giving background information about the branch and for arranging attendance at branch meetings. All the fully qualified members in the five branches were contacted in the first place. Since the number of these was rather small (28), an equal number of semi-qualified members (H.N.C.) was also selected, according to their proportions in the respective branches. These comprised over 76 per cent of this group.

In the event several of them were found to have left the union or the area (the secretary's records being out of date), and a few had recently become fully qualified. There were three refusals, all of them qualified members, so that those interviewed finally consisted of 28 qualified and 21 semi-qualified members. Few of these respondents had a telephone, and most of them were contacted by letter in the way described above.

These two sets of respondents cannot really be considered as samples. They comprise only very small proportions, around 1 per cent, of their respective bodies. The information obtained refers strictly only to the Merseyside area. This is almost certainly not representative of the whole country in many respects, but is perhaps less so as far as the members of these two bodies are concerned. Of course, even apart from any geographical bias, it is possible with such small numbers that chance factors could produce bias. These reservations must be borne in mind, but they are not believed to create overwhelming objections.

## The Questionnaire and Interview Schedules

The questionnaire and the two schedules were basically similar. The first questions dealt with date of birth, educational experience, qualifications, present employer, official position and type of work performed. The next dealt with date of joining the body, the reason for doing so, opinions on its most important functions, services used and suggestions for other activities. The Guild members were then asked whether they thought all engineers should join, and the A.Sc.W. members whether they considered collective bargaining as suitable. Both were next asked their views on why others had not joined. The A.Sc.W. members were also asked whether they thought there was any necessary connection between trade unionism and politics, and whether they would be willing to hold office in the branch.

The next set of questions dealt with satisfaction or otherwise with four aspects of their work: the use made of knowledge and skill, status, opportunities for promotion, and salary. In the case of the postal questionnaire respondents were asked to record their degree of satisfaction when comparing themselves first with metallurgists, and secondly with other groups. All were then asked whether they thought their association should do more about any of these things, and if so, what. In the case

# METHODS USED IN THE STUDY

of the Guild there was next a question on their views about collective bargaining, and finally, for all three bodies, a request for any further comments. With the personal interviews the wording of the questions on the schedules was closely, but not strictly, adhered to.

# Index

# INDEX

# INDEX

Pike, R. M., 21n
Postgate, R. W., 145n
Price, D. J., 23
Price, D. K., 26
Professionalism:
  Definition, 44–47, 61–62
  Functions, 65–82, 87–92, 176–82
  History, 63–65
  and Status, 31, 43–47, 61–62, 65,
    178–82

Rattan, V. W., 17n
Reissman, L., 31, 32n
Rex, J., 36n
Ricardo, 32
Riegel, J. W., 163n, 164n
Robbins Report, 85n
Royal Commission on Doctors' and
  Dentists' Remuneration, 77
Royal Institute of Chemistry, 20,
  53, 64, 68, 69, 73, 74, 76, 77, 78,
  81
Royal Institution of British Archi-
  tects, 72
Royal Institution of Naval Archi-
  tects, 64
Royal Society, 25, 27

Sampson, A., 25n, 26, 28n
Schilling, W. R., 27
Schumpeter, J. A., 36n
Scientists:
  Attitudes, 159–70
  Earnings, 53–58, 176
  Education, 158–59
  Employment, 21–24, 48–52, 150–
    154, 158, 175–6
  and Politics, 25–28
  and Society, 17–20
Scott, C., 190n
Scott, W. H., 17n
Shils, E., 28n
Smiles, S., 64n
Snow, C. P., 18, 26
Society of Civil Engineers, 63
Society of Engineers, 64, 75
Status:
  and Class, 35–38

Consciousness, 41–42, 95, 112–14,
  117, 121, 124, 170, 174
  and Legitimacy, 36–37
  and Professionalism, 31, 43–47,
    175, 178–82
  Theory, 34–35, 173–5
Stephenson, George, 64, 67

Textile Institute, 71, 72n
*The Times*, 21
Trade Union Act, 141, 183
Trade Union Congress, 131, 134,
  135, 137, 138, 144, 165, 183
Transport Salaried Staffs Associa-
  tion, 135, 141
Trend Report, 24
Tropp, A., 132n
Tudsbury, J. H. T., 63n

Unionism:
  in Central government, 129–30,
    143, 146–7, 182
  and Class, 31, 42–44, 169–70,
    183–5
  in Education, 132–3, 182
  in Local government, 130–2,
    143, 146–7, 182
  in Nationalized industry, 133–5,
    143, 146–7, 182
  in Private industry, 135–40, 147–
    148, 150–4, 182–3
  Professional (nature), 140–5,
    159–70
  and Professional associations, 78–
    80, 102, 106, 112–15, 118–21
Union of Shop, Distributive and
  Allied Workers, 156
United Kingdom Atomic Energy
  Authority, 49, 55, 56, 120, 134

Walton, R. E., 140n, 142n, 161n
Warner, L., 30n, 35n
Weber, M., 16, 32, 35, 36
White, L. D., 129n
Wilson, P. A., 44, 63n, 64n, 68n,
  72n, 73n, 74, 76n, 79n, 133
Withey, S. B., 18n

Zuckerman, Sir Solly, 25, 26